Edexcel GCSE

History
Controlled Assessment

CA11 Change in British society 1955–75

Nigel Bushnell and Cathy Warren
Series editor: Angela Leonard

A PEARSON COMPANY

Introduction

This unit is about how and why British society changed in the years c.1955–c.1975. You will see that immigration and the liberalisation of society, often involving changes in the law, altered the face of British society.

You will also see that the rate and extent of change varied in different parts of the country and between different social groups. People's experiences differed from each other, depending on their personal situation and the social influences on them. Although there is a great deal of evidence of radical change in many aspects of life, many attitudes were slow to change and changed at a different pace in different parts of the country or for different sections of society.

Part A of this book covers:

○ immigration

○ sex discrimination and the changing role of women

○ the liberalisation of society

○ the 'swinging sixties'.

For your controlled assessment in this unit, you will learn how to carry out an enquiry (Part A) and to analyse and evaluate representations of history (Part B). Later sections of this book cover the skills you will need to be successful in unit 4.

Your Part A enquiry will focus in detail on one key question. In Part B you will focus on representations of history: how to analyse, compare and evaluate different views of the 'swinging sixties'.

Contents

Change in British society 1955–75

Part A: Carry out a historical enquiry

Part B: Representations of history

Part A Carry out a historical enquiry

A1 Immigration

Learning outcomes

By the end of this topic, you should be able to:

- explain Britain's need for more workers after the Second World War, and the encouragement of immigration
- analyse the experience of immigrants in Britain from c.1955 to c.1975
- understand the role of the government in both limiting immigration and in trying to improve race relations.

Colonies: territories which were part of the British Empire.

Commonwealth: after gaining independence, some former British colonies joined this association. 'New Commonwealth' referred to the mainly non-white and developing areas of the British Commonwealth in Africa and Asia, and 'Old Commonwealth' to areas such as Canada, Australia and New Zealand, which had gained independence earlier.

A key feature of Britain since the Second World War has been the development of a multiracial society. Immediately after the Second World War some leading political figures from both the Conservative and Labour parties had spoken proudly of Britain's recent fight against the racism of Nazi Germany. They said Britain was different. Britain was unique. Britain was a place where different races could live and work harmoniously together. But was this really true?

Before the Second World War there were very few black and even fewer Asian people in Britain itself although many black and Asian men from the colonies served in the British armed forces during the war. After the Second World War, the 1948 British Nationality Act gave all 800 million people in the **Commonwealth** the right to claim British citizenship. This meant that they could come and live in Britain – the 'mother country' – without any visa requirements. There were no government controls or restrictions on immigration from the Commonwealth until 1962.

From the mid-1950s until 1961, around 30,000 people a year were emigrating from the 'New Commonwealth' to Britain.

The British Commonwealth: this map shows 'Old' Commonwealth countries and some of the 'New' Commonwealth countries which joined after 1945.

Old Commonwealth
New Commonwealth

Did you know?

In 1950 there were only six Indian restaurants in the whole of Britain. Within one generation, by 1970, there would be 2,000 and curry was set to become Britain's favourite meal!

Why was there so much immigration into Britain in the 1950s?

- **Recruitment campaigns by British firms:** There were big recruitment campaigns for workers in the National Health Service, which had only recently been established, in 1948. Many textile firms in northern England recruited workers from India and Pakistan. London Transport actually went to the Caribbean to search for staff. In 1956 alone, for example, 140 staff were employed by London Transport from a recruiting office set up in Barbados. London Transport itself became widely recognised as making a significant contribution to race relations. Many black immigrants soon gained management jobs.

- **Shortage of labour:** The most practical reason for post-war immigration was that, by the 1950s, Britain had a serious shortage of labour. The government and many private companies found some jobs very difficult to fill. Most of the shortages were for low-paid and unskilled workers.

Source A: London Transport officials in Barbados in 1954 recruiting staff for buses and trains.

- **Opportunities for immigrants:** Many viewed working in Britain, the 'mother country', as an opportunity to earn good wages. Most earlier immigrants were male and aimed to work in Britain for a short period while sending money back to their families, before returning back 'home' themselves.

- **Encouragement and support for immigrants:** Some migrating to Britain were given an interest-free loan from their own government for travel costs. London Transport provided hostels for many of the immigrants it recruited.

Activities

1. What do you understand by the term 'mother country'?

2. Look at Source A. Can you think of three hopes and three fears the young black men in the picture may have had about emigrating to Britain?

Follow up your enquiry

Research the significance of a ship called the *Windrush* for immigration to Britain after the Second World War.

The experience of immigrants 1955–1975

But for many immigrants, Britain was not as welcoming as they had expected. Those migrating to Britain often settled in the poorer inner-city areas of cities such as London, Birmingham and Bradford.

Increasingly these districts became areas with relatively high immigrant populations – such as Brixton in south London, Handsworth in Birmingham and Toxteth in Liverpool. Often, the white people in these areas began to move out to other parts of the city. By 1957 the government was concerned at what was described as 'white-flight' and 'segregation' in some of Britain's major towns and cities.

Tensions started to develop within these mainly white working-class communities. Some trade unions complained about immigrants taking jobs from whites by accepting work at lower wages. Some politicians and some of the British public argued that, instead of coming to Britain to work, many were coming to Britain simply to receive generous welfare benefits. Tensions also developed about education and housing.

However, the experiences of many immigrants were often very different.

- Some were highly educated but were forced to take on low-skilled employment. This was often because their qualifications were not recognised in Britain.
- Many found themselves sharing overcrowded and substandard accommodation.
- 'No coloureds' and 'No blacks' could often be seen on signs for accommodation or in advertisements for job vacancies.

There were some other social reasons which also increased racial mistrust. Many of the early immigrants were young men without their families with them in Britain.

- A culture of drinking in bars and clubs with modern music, gambling, drug-taking and prostitution began to develop among immigrants.

Source B: A sign reading no Irish, no blacks, no dogs' displayed in a British guest house window in the early 1960s.

- By the late 1950s, many young white working-class 'Teddy Boys' were beginning to attack black immigrants who they thought were taking 'their women' and graffiti appeared such as 'Keep Britain white'.
- Some newspapers published sensationalised and exaggerated reports about the supposed lack of cleanliness, criminal activities and sexual practices of immigrants in Britain.

The increasing numbers of Asian immigrants settling in Britain faced additional problems.

- They often spoke a different language and understood little English, which meant that finding work was difficult.
- They often practised very different religious customs, such as arranged marriages and fasting. This meant that they were excluded from many social activities, such as those which involved alcohol.

These circumstances meant Asian immigrants were more likely to try to set up their own businesses, and often bought cheaper property in rundown areas and then rented it out to later immigrants.

Activities

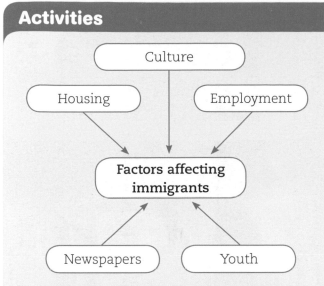

3. In groups of five, each person should take one of the five factors shown on the chart above. For each factor they should explain how it affected the experience of many immigrants in Britain in the 1950s. Each of the five reports should then be used to make a presentation to the whole class on 'Immigration to Britain in the 1950s'

4. Draw a horizontal line across the middle of a double page. Title the chart 'The impact of immigration.' On one end write 'positive' and on the other end put 'negative'. Create a series of statements and plot them where you think they belong along the spectrum. Here are two statements for you to start with:

   • 'No blacks' and 'No coloureds' signs in windows during the 1950s.

   • High proportion of Asian immigrants setting up their own businesses.

The Notting Hill race riots, 1958

In 1958 there were race riots in both Nottingham and London. In Nottingham on the night of 23 August 1958, almost 1,000 white and black youths fought each other and a number of stabbings occurred. These were followed by riots in August 1958 in Notting Hill, London, which received widespread news coverage – both within Britain and worldwide.

In the Notting Hill area of west London a strong Caribbean community had developed. There was, however, widespread poverty in both the white and the 'new' Caribbean households. The situation was also made worse in the area by a number of landlords who had evicted long-term white residents from properties and then re-let the same property to newly arrived immigrants at much higher rents.

Over a period of almost two weeks in August 1958 in Notting Hill, hundreds of young, white men with chains, knives, iron bars and petrol bombs attacked groups of black immigrants and their homes with chants such as 'niggers out'. More than a hundred white men were arrested as well as some black men who had armed themselves in self-defence.

Source C: Police officers arresting a white demonstrator during the Notting Hill riots, 1958.

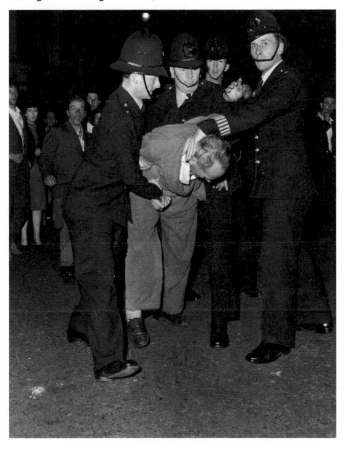

Overall, British public opinion was shocked by the events at Notting Hill. Much of the British public had seen television news coverage of the police trying to keep black and white groups apart, and firefighters putting out fires caused by petrol bombs being thrown. In many ways the Notting Hill riots were a turning point:

- There was some resentment and anger from the black community as many felt that at the time the police purposely downplayed the racial element of the riots.
- After the Notting Hill riots more than 4,000 immigrants returned to the Caribbean.
- An official complaint was made by Caribbean governments to the British government.
- Both political and public opinion became very divided. *The Times* commented on 'the ugliest fighting' whereas the *Daily Mail* asked its readers 'Should we let them carry on coming in?'
- Immigrant groups in Britain became more organised. The Organisation for the Protection of Coloured People was set up. There was also, for example, a rent strike in Notting Hill by some immigrants until repairs were carried out on their housing.

Official government reports commented on the reluctance of local factories to take on black workers and also on the racial tensions created due to the relationships between black men and white women.

There now began a series of debates about the extent of immigration to British inner cities and how to deal with racial tension and racism. At national government level policies on immigration had to deal with two main issues:

- the numbers of immigrants entering Britain
- methods to tackle racial discrimination.

The first issue was always going to be more straightforward, but still controversial for the government to deal with.

Source D: Protestors in Notting Hill in 1959.

Activities

5. Complete a table, using the headings below, to show the main features of the 1958 Notting Hill riots:

   Causes → Events → Effects

6. Take on the role of an advisor to the government on race relations. Following the Notting Hill riots what are your key recommendations for preventing further riots like those in Notting Hill in 1958?

7. 'After the Notting Hill riots of 1958 Britain could no longer claim to be a "mother country"'. Do you agree? Explain your answer.

Dealing with the numbers of immigrants entering Britain

Both Conservative and Labour politicians wanted to avoid upsetting Britain's relations with Commonwealth governments, but at the same time there were serious concerns about the effects of immigration on British society. The Conservative Party, led by Harold Macmillan, won the general election in 1959 at a time when there was increasing pressure on the government to restrict immigration. The general public seemed increasingly opposed to Britain's lack of controls on immigration. Public opinion often included comments such as 'send them back home' or 'no more in this country'.

In 1961 there was a sudden increase in immigration to Britain (see table below) which was partly because some feared the British government was making preparations to limit the numbers allowed to enter the country.

Immigration into Britain from the New Commonwealth 1956–1962

	Caribbean	India, Pakistan and Bangladesh	Total
1956	26,000	8,000	34,000
1957	23,000	7,000	30,000
1958	17,000	11,000	28,000
1959	20,000	4,000	24,000
1960	53,000	10,000	63,000
1961	62,000	50,000	112,000
1962	35,000	47,000	82,000

Laws to control immigration

Commonwealth Immigrants Act 1962

Politicians were very divided on the issue of restricting immigration. Nonetheless, in 1962 the first Commonwealth Immigrants Act was passed, which applied to former British colonies.

This Act meant that immigrants from those colonies needed to have prearranged a job before entering Britain or have special skills that were needed by the British economy. This was controlled through issuing 'employment vouchers'.

The effects of the 1962 Commonwealth Immigrants Act:

- Some claimed that the Act itself was racist as most of Britain's former colonies were in Asia, Africa and the Caribbean.
- Some opinion polls claimed that nearly three quarters of the British public supported the controls on immigration.
- It encouraged many immigrants already in Britain to remain permanently rather than returning home. Many feared that, if they left Britain at that point, they would be unable to return at a later date.
- It meant that many immigrants already in Britain would be more likely to be joined by their families.
- It was now clear that non-white immigration was seen by the government as a problem that needed to be solved.

The 1962 Commonwealth Immigrants Act was followed by even tighter controls.

Commonwealth Immigrants Act 1968

As well as needing an employment voucher, this meant that immigrants also needed to have a parent or grandparent who had been born in Britain.

Immigration Act 1971

This replaced employment vouchers with 12-month work permits so that immigrants could only remain in Britain for a limited period of time.

By the early 1970s Britain had stopped virtually all black and Asian **primary immigration** to Britain. Britain now had some of the toughest immigration laws in the world.

> **Primary immigration:** refers to a person moving to Britain alone. If members of their family join them later, this is called secondary immigration.

Activities

8. Copy and complete the chart below to show the key features of the three Immigration Acts in this period. For each Act, give it a rating out of ten on how effective you think the Act was for the two main issues.

Act	Meeting the concerns of those against immigration	Improving race relations in Britain
1962 Commonwealth Immigrants Act		
1968 Commonwealth Immigrants Act		
1971 Immigration Act		

9. Choose one of the Immigration Acts. In pairs write one newspaper editorial which supports the Act and one editorial which criticises the Act.

Political opposition to immigration

From the late 1950s onwards, race and immigration increasingly became fiercely debated issues within national politics.

In the 1959 general election, Oswald Mosley campaigned as the parliamentary candidate for the Kensington North constituency, which included the Notting Hill area. Mosley had set up the British Union of **Fascists** in 1932 and had been imprisoned by the British Government during the Second World War because his fascist views and links to the Nazi Party meant that he was believed to be a threat to national security. His main campaign in 1959 was against immigration to Britain. He gained only 8 per cent of the vote.

In the 1964 general election, the Conservative candidate for Smethwick in Birmingham, Peter Griffiths, defeated the Labour MP. Griffiths had even used the slogan 'if you want a nigger for a neighbour vote Labour'.

Outside of the major political parties, the National Front Party was formed in 1967. It firmly opposed immigration as well as any measures to improve race relations and multiculturalism. It had a mainly working-class membership of 20,000 by the mid-1970s. There was widespread shock when the National Front won 16 per cent of the vote in a by-election in West Bromwich, Birmingham in 1973. Although it failed to gain any parliamentary seats, it was more well-known for raising tension with noisy demonstrations and marches. It was an almost non-existent organisation by the late 1970s.

Enoch Powell

In 1968, Enoch Powell, a Conservative MP in the Shadow Cabinet, made a speech to a Conservative Association meeting which famously highlighted the race issue. Powell felt that immigration was a direct threat to British national identity and warned of what he saw as a violent future for British multiracial society if the numbers of immigrants continued unchecked. His speech, which became known as the 'Rivers of Blood speech', argued for an end to any further non-white immigration and for the introduction of **voluntary repatriation**.

Voluntary repatriation: when individuals choose to return to the country of their origin of their own free will. It may be organised with or without the government's assistance.

Fascist: relating to a political movement or party which believes that nation and race are more important than the individual. Fascist systems have an all-powerful central government and an authoritarian leader.

Source E: Enoch Powell, MP, speaking in 1968.

Source F: London Dock workers marching to the Houses of Parliament in support of Enoch Powell in April 1968.

The speech made Powell both hated and popular at the same time. Some members of the Conservative Party felt he had gone too far and threatened to resign unless Powell was made to resign. The day after the speech, the Conservative Party leader, Edward Heath, sacked Powell from the Shadow Cabinet. Heath also made a public statement to say that the speech would increase racial tensions. Powell never held a senior government position again – even though he had been regarded by some as a future leader of the Conservative Party.

But Powell received a lot of popular support especially from the working class. There were marches by London dock workers in support of him. Their march to Parliament included chants of 'Bye bye blackbird' and placards with slogans such as 'Back Britain not black Britain'. A campaign to stop Powell being sacked gathered a petition of over 30,000 signatures and the London dockers even threatened strike action in support of Powell. Opinion polls at the time suggested that 75 per cent of the British public agreed with Enoch Powell's speech. This was against a background of increased attacks on non-whites and their property.

Activity

10. Draw a graph to show racial tension in Britain during the period 1955 to 1975. Label the vertical axis as 'tension' and then divide the horizontal axis to cover 1955 to 1975. Mark key events on the graph (such as the Notting Hill riots, Powell's 'Rivers of Blood' speech). Now draw a line to show how you think racial tension in Britain increased and decreased during this period.

ResultsPlus
Top Tip

When carrying out your research into race relations, don't forget that riots and demonstrations were the result of the actions of a relatively small number of individuals.

Dealing with racism in Britain

Government policies were introduced which aimed to ease racial integration and deal with racism.

The Race Relations Act 1965, introduced by Labour **Home Secretary** Roy Jenkins, led to the setting up of the Race Relations Board, and was followed by the Race Relations Act 1968. From then on:

- discrimination in housing and employment was banned
- the 'colour bar' in public places was banned. This made illegal the use of restrictions such as 'no coloureds' and 'Europeans only' used by some landlords and employers
- incitement to racial hatred was banned.

The Race Relations Board dealt with complaints about racial discrimination. However, the Race Relations Board was seen to have very limited success:

- It could not be used to bring up complaints about the police.
- Only about 10 per cent of complaints to the Race Relations Board were ever upheld and, therefore, many saw it as a waste of their time to try to make a formal complaint.

Source G: An extract from the Bernie Grant archives, held at Middlesex University. Bernie Grant was elected MP for the London constituency of Tottenham in 1987 – one of only three black MPs in Britain at the time. He first came to Britain in 1963 when he was 19 years old.

> When I arrived here there were still the signs on the windows – no blacks, no Irish, no dogs, no children. Then there was the Race Relations Act of 1968, which outlawed all that. But what I found was that the problem lay in this institutional racism, hidden policies [of racial discrimination in important organisations including those run by the government] which you found in housing, in education and so on. There would be a policy which said that to get a house you needed such and such connections with the borough. Then they would define 'connections' as having your family living there for three generations or whatever. It was moving the goalposts, and it meant that black families hadn't a hope of getting a house. There were many policies in education that discriminated against black people. It was easy enough to deal with overt [clear and open] racism; you could fight the people concerned and that would be the end of it. The institutionalised variety just kept going. So I became involved with a lot of anti-racist work.

Follow up your enquiry

Research one of the following topics:
- the life of Bernie Grant – and write his biography
- when Britain had its first black and Asian MPs and how many there are in parliament today.

Home Secretary: the government minister in charge of the Home Office of the UK, responsible for many important issues such as policing, immigration and national security.

Activities

11. What does Source G tell you about the effects that the 1968 Race Relations Act had on ordinary black British lives in the early 1970s?

12. In Source G, Bernie Grant uses the terms 'overt' and 'institutionalised' racism. Complete a table such as the one below with three examples of each of these types of racism.

Overt racism	Institutionalised racism

13. Make a display titled 'Race relations in Britain 1955–1975'. You could use a double page divided into two or a PowerPoint™ presentation. Use images which would fit under the title 'Racism in Britain' and another set of images which would fit under the title 'Multiracial Britain'.

Multiracial Britain by the mid-1970s

By the mid-1970s, Asian and black communities were a familiar and established feature of British society. The west London site where riots and racism had taken place in 1958 was now the site of a vibrant and annual celebration – the Notting Hill Carnival. In fact, the carnival was begun in 1959 in the year immediately after the Notting Hill riots. It was set up with the express aim of uniting the black and white working-class communities at a time when race relations were at a very low point. Initially it was held indoors and then moved to the streets of Notting Hill in 1966.

By the mid-1970s there was more integration between white people and immigrants. A new, second generation of British-born immigrants, attending British schools and adopting British culture, was developing. This often brought with it another set of tensions. First-generation immigrants often felt their children were losing their racial identity, customs and traditions. Many of these issues were dealt with in an award-winning comedy, *East is East*, made in 1999. It is set in Manchester in the early 1970s in a household with a father from Pakistan and an English mother from Manchester. The father expects his children to follow strict Pakistani traditions, but the children born in England increasingly reject their father's rules on food, religion and life in general.

ResultsPlus

Top Tip

Always try to back up the points you make, using specific and precise information.

Source H: **A photograph of the Notting Hill Carnival, 1971.**

Follow up your enquiry

Research the history of the Notting Hill Carnival.

The role of the media in changing attitudes

There was a gradual easing of racial tension in Britain by the mid-1970s. Some of this was partly due to the media taking a role in trying to influence people's attitudes and encouraging greater acceptance. Films and television played their part too:

- **1967: British-made film, *To Sir With Love***
  This was a major success in British cinemas. The film is about an educated black man in London who accepts a job as teacher in a tough, mainly white, school.

- **1972–76: popular BBC sitcom, *Love Thy Neighbour***
  The main characters are a white couple trying to come to terms with their black neighbours. The white male was scripted to look ignorant compared to his more accepting wife. In contrast the black male character is far more educated but also uses racism. The white and black women get on well together.

- **1965-75: popular BBC sitcom, *Til Death Us Do Part***
  The main character was a white, working-class man who expressed racist views which made him appear ridiculous. (However, many viewers shared the character's views and missed the point that he was being mocked.)

The role of the government in changing attitudes

Although the Race Relations Acts of the 1960s did not stop racial discrimination, they did mean there was an official government statement on values in British society, which was an important step in the move forward to a multicultural society.

The Labour Home Secretary, James Callaghan, commented on the Acts as a way of creating 'a society in which, although the government might control who came in, once they were in, they should be treated equally'.

From 1976 onwards, tougher government laws were passed which:

- made racial discrimination illegal
- gave tougher powers to prosecute by extending discrimination to include victimisation
- enabled closer supervision of the work of the police.

> **Legislation:** laws made by a government or ruling body.

 Your conclusion so far

From this topic we have seen that:

- Both the government and the public changed their views on race in Britain.
- These changes took a long time and, at various points between 1965 and 1975, race was a very emotive topic, both in government and in Britain as a whole.
- The government has continually aimed to restrict the numbers of immigrants while at the same time wanting to protect the rights of, and raise opportunities for, immigrants in Britain.

From what you have learned in this topic so far, to what extent do you think Britain was becoming a society where different races could live alongside each other harmoniously by the mid-1970s?

To answer this question, first make a table with two columns headed 'Race relations in Britain in 1955' and 'Race relations in Britain in 1975', then list the changes in race relations in Britain during this 20-year period.

Include:

- The changing treatment of immigrants in Britain by the government and through **legislation**.
- The changing social attitudes towards immigration.
- The role of some individuals who have tried to respond to or even reverse these changes.

Decide how much you think the issue of race changed in Britain between the mid-1950s and the mid-1970s.

A2 Sex discrimination and the changing role of women

Learning outcomes

By the end of this topic, you should be able to:

- understand the changing role of women in Britain 1955–1975 (what they could actually do, both in the home and at work)
- understand the changing status of women in Britain 1955–1975 (how they were regarded and how important they were)
- examine the roles of the government, the women's movement and other individuals in bringing about these changes
- evaluate the extent of real change to women's lives in Britain by 1975.

During the Second World War (1939–1945), the employment of women in Britain had been at its peak. As well as being employed in factories and in agriculture, women played a vital role in Britain's armed forces.

But, after the war, the number of women in work fell by nearly two million, and British society returned to very traditional gender roles.

Thus many of the gains made by women during the Second World War, in terms of both their roles and status in society, were only temporary.

It may be quite hard to imagine what it was like for the majority of women in Britain before the 1960s. For example, women would have found it difficult to get a mortgage and even needed a man to guarantee items bought on **hire purchase**. In many ways the role and status of women in Britain changed during the 1960s and 1970s.

Hire purchase: paying an initial deposit for items (such as furniture, cars or clothes) followed by monthly payments with interest over an agreed period.

A summary of the changes in the position of women in Britain from the 1950s to the 1970s

	Women in Britain in the 1950s	Women in Britain in the 1970s
	It was usual for women to give up work as soon as they got married.	It was not assumed women would give up work when they got married.
	It was generally accepted that the woman's primary responsibility was for the home and childcare. Working women would be seen as neglecting these duties.	It was more acceptable for women to work, although they still remained responsible for the home and childcare.
	Women who did work often earned two-thirds of the amount earned by men for doing exactly the same job.	After 1975, the law required that women receive the same pay as men for the same sort of work.
	Women made up a quarter of students at British universities.	Women made up nearly a half of students at British universities.
	No woman had been a leader of a British political party.	In 1975 Margaret Thatcher became the first female leader of a British political party – the Conservative Party.

These changes in the position of women in society were due to a combination of:

- changing social attitudes towards marriage and the family
- increasing educational and employment opportunities for women, creating the momentum for further changes
- women's protest movements campaigning for more gender equality and increased legal protection for women
- government legislation to give greater gender equality and rights for women.

However, there were limits to the amount of change in the role and status of women in Britain between the mid-1950s and the mid-1970s. Some men and women still held very traditional attitudes towards women in both the home and the workplace.

- The proportion of women in certain professions and careers was still very low.
- In many careers women seemed less likely than men to be promoted and to hold one of the 'top' jobs.

Activity

1. Copy the diagram showing the factors involved in the changing role of women in Britain between the 1950s and the 1970s. On the diagram show how the factors are interlinked.

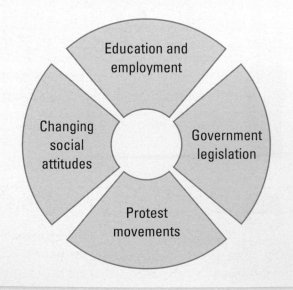

Activity

"What's it going to be, Dawkins—career or family?"

2. This cartoon from the early 1970s shows a woman at a meeting in work with young children being shouted at by her boss: 'What's it going to be, Dawkins – career or family?' What does it tell you about attitudes to women at this time?

Results**Plus**

Top Tip

Students who can show how factors link together and explain their importance can gain the highest marks in Part A of the controlled assessment.

For most of the 1950s and 1960s, the role and status of women in Britain was very traditional. In the 1950s and 1960s:

- the average age of getting married was 22 years old
- nearly a third of all women were still teenagers when they got married
- for most women marriage meant the traditional role as wife and mother: working in the home looking after their husband and children
- nearly two thirds of all births in the 1960s were to women under the age of 25.

During the 1960s and early 1970s there was a significant growth in both household amenities and domestic appliances. In many ways these reduced both the physical and time demands of running the home.

- By the late 1960s most British households had running water, gas and electricity.

- Fridges and cookers were no longer seen as luxury items.

- Household appliances such as washing machines and freezers were becoming more common.

- Shopping patterns were changing with a rapid increase in 'one-stop' supermarkets which reduced the time needed for shopping. The number of supermarkets in Britain grew from around 300 in the mid-1960s to more than 5,000 by the early 1970s.

- Shopping from home began to develop with shopping through catalogues and mail-order services.

But, did these developments in the range of household goods available and new patterns of shopping significantly alter the traditional role and status of women?

- New household goods were often only affordable by middle-class households and therefore did not have such an impact on working-class homes.

- Supermarket and home-shopping catalogues often used advertising images and messages which continued to reinforce the domestic role of women.

- Women's magazines often reinforced traditional social attitudes with messages such as 'happy family', 'keeping your man', and 'be more beautiful'.

Source A: An extract from *The New Look*, by Harry Hopkins, published in 1964.

> The female kitchen is the temple of those twin symbols of the new life – the refrigerator and the washing machine. It is the heart of the feminine dream, full of gadgetry, whirring and wires.

Source B: An advertisement in a catalogue for home furnishings from the mid-1960s.

Activity

3. How do Sources A and B reflect the traditional roles of women?

Follow up your enquiry

Research advertising used in the 1960s by supermarkets and mail-order companies. What messages do the advertisements give about the role of women?

Education and employment of women

In the mid-1950s most careers and professions were almost entirely male dominated. This was due to a combination of:

- women's educational opportunities
- social attitudes towards marriage and family life
- employment patterns.

Examinations called the '11 plus' were taken by most primary school children across Britain until the mid-1970s. Those children who passed went to grammar schools, where the education was more academic. An equal numbers of boys and girls attended these higher-attaining schools. However, girls' educational opportunities at the end of compulsory schooling were limited.

- The vast majority of working-class girls left school at the minimum school-leaving age. This was 15 until 1972, when it was raised to 16.
- Even though girls who did take 'O-level' examinations at 16 (the equivalent of today's GCSEs) did as well as boys, very few continued in education to study for A-levels.
- Those girls who did stay on at school after the minimum school-leaving age often went to college to study in areas such as secretarial skills, childcare, or hairdressing.
- Even fewer women went to university. In the early 1960s women made up only a quarter of undergraduate students. Very few women studied science, engineering, medicine or law.
- For the small proportion of women who did study at university, many found themselves marrying soon after finishing their degree. They then began a family and took on the traditional female role as a housewife and mother.

This obviously then restricted employment and career opportunities for most women. For those women who did work, the combination of social attitudes, limited education and lack of government legislation meant that in the 1950s and 1960s their employment opportunities were very restricted.

Factors restricting women's employment in Britain in the 1950s and 1960s

Social attitudes towards the family	Many still felt that working women were selfish and neglecting their responsibilities in the home. There were very few affordable childminders, so working-class women often relied on family and friends. Nursery education was expensive and was therefore an option only for wealthier families.
Limited education	Girls' limited educational opportunities meant that women were often restricted to lower-paid and lower-skilled employment sectors. In the 1960s, 80 per cent of all secretarial, shop and factory work was done by women. Only 15 per cent of doctors and 5 per cent of the law profession were women.
Lack of government legislation	Women applying for jobs often found employers were reluctant to appoint them to responsible positions because it was assumed women would marry and would need to leave work once they had a family. When women did have the same jobs as men they generally received lower pay. Employers also often argued that women returning to work would be unwilling to work long hours and would need to take time off work if their children were ill.

Source C: A page in a 'Peter and Jane' reading book, from a series commonly used to teach young children to read from the early 1950s to the late 1960s.

6

Jane likes to help Mummy. She wants to make cakes like Mummy.

"Let me help you, Mummy," she says. "Will you let me help, please? I can make cakes like you."

"Yes," says Mummy, "I will let you help me. You are a good girl."

"We will make some cakes for Peter and Daddy," says Jane. "They like the cakes we make."

new words

let   will

Activities

4. In groups of three or four carry out a role-play of an employer interviewing people for a job in the early 1960s. The candidates should include at least one young man and one young woman. The employer should explain which person successfully got the job.

5. Look at the table of women's employment statistics. What can you learn from this about changes to women's employment in Britain? What can't you tell from these statistics about changes to women's employment in Britain?

Women in paid employment in Britain 1951–1971

	1951	1961	1971
Women as percentage of total workforce	30	35	40
Percentage of all married women aged 15–59 who work	25	35	50

ResultsPlus

Top Tip

To show that something has changed, make clear comparisons. You should use words such as 'before' or 'after' or give dates: 'in the 1950s… but by the 1970s…'.

Follow up your enquiry

Research and watch extracts of the film *Educating Rita*, about a working-class woman's desire for education and 'betterment'. What does the film tell you about social attitudes towards women and married life in Britain in the 1970s?

Did you know?

The 'Women's Liberation' movement calculated that women spent on average 40 hours a week doing housework and walked more than 50 miles a week doing household work.

The growth of feminism and the Women's Liberation movement

The National Housewives' Register began in 1960. Developed as an organisation for 'housebound wives', it was originally called the 'Housebound Wives' Register' and is now the NWR (National Women's Register). This organisation was involved in the setting up of local branches for women to join. They generally met in each other's homes, as well as arranging days out and an annual national conference. By the mid-1970s it had 20,000 members. This organisation reflected the boredom and frustration felt by many middle-class women in particular.

The actual role and status of women was changed more because of the growth of feminist ideas and the Women's Liberation movement. Much of the influence of the movement and feminist ideas came from the women's groups campaigning in the United States of America and the work of Betty Friedan, who published her book *The Feminine Mystique* in 1963.

From the late 1960s onwards, feminist movements began to emerge in Britain. **Feminism** covered a whole range of various beliefs but its main aims were to challenge social attitudes as well as to establish more rights and legal protection for women.

By the 1970s, the Women's Liberation movement had become a national movement with groups in most British towns, cities and universities.

In 1970 the first Women's National Liberation Conference was held in Oxford. The movement put together four key demands:

- equal pay for men and women
- equal education and career opportunities for men and women
- free contraception and abortion on demand
- freely available 24-hour childcare.

Feminist ideas challenged the traditional roles and status of women, who showed their frustration at what they saw as the slow rate of social change.

> **Feminism:** a movement and set of beliefs aimed at achieving political, social and economic equality of women with men.

Source D: The National Women's Liberation Movement march in London, 1971.

The feminist argument

> Traditional gender roles meant that women remained in the home as wives and mothers.

> This meant that men were at work, earning money and therefore had much more social and economic power.

> Therefore the traditional domestic position of women had to be challenged first.

> Then the wider discrimination faced by women in education and employment could be fought.

> Changes in law would also be necessary to make sexism and stereotyping an offence which could be legally challenged.

The campaign for greater sexual equality and to challenge sexism used various methods to spread its message.

Protests

Women's Liberation groups also organised marches which included the burning of bras and chants such as 'We're not beautiful; we're not ugly; we're angry!' Such direct action followed the symbolic act when American women had ceremonially binned their bras outside the Miss America pageant in 1968.

In November 1970 women demonstrated at the Miss World contest at the Royal Albert Hall, London. They saw the competition as reinforcing sexism. The women shouted, threw flour, stink bombs and leaflets onto the stage and constantly heckled the presenter. This led to several arrests and some women were fined.

Publications

A range of books which expressed new ideas about women's liberation were published. One of the most influential was Germaine Greer's *The Female Eunuch*, published in 1970. It argued that women were repressed by their role in the home, the social ideal of the **nuclear family** and by increasing consumerism. Its radical views and the deliberate use of crude language caused something of an explosion and led to some husbands banning their wives from reading it.

> **Nuclear family:** a family unit of two married parents and their children in one household.

Key individuals

The feminist movement also had the support of influential women at the time. Barbara Castle and Shirley Williams held various ministerial posts under the Labour Prime Minister, Harold Wilson. Vanessa Redgrave was a very prominent British actress who openly supported political campaigns in the 1960s and 1970s such as the Campaign for Nuclear Disarmament and protest against the Vietnam War.

Opposition

Opponents of Women's Liberation often argued that:

- working women did not have the time to raise their children properly – so they were seen by some as responsible for youth crime
- women could not cope with the pressures and demands of the workplace
- women campaigning for more equality were 'unfeminine' and bitter at being unable to 'find the right man'.

Activities

6. What do you understand by the term 'women's liberation'?

7. Look at the four demands on page 19 made by Women's Liberation groups in Britain. Rank them in what you think should be the order of importance and explain your reasons.

The fight for equal pay

The most symbolic and successful women's protest was by working-class women at Ford car factories in 1968.

From the mid-1950s onwards, the government had gradually started introducing equal pay for men and women in teaching, the civil service and local government. From the mid-1960s onwards there was increasing pressure for equal pay for men and women in other areas of employment.

In 1968, working-class women, working as sewing machinists at Ford car plants in Halewood in Liverpool and Dagenham in East London, went on strike.

- They went on strike to have their pay regraded. The strike successfully brought about the closure of both the Dagenham and Halewood factories for three weeks.
- Their work making seat covers and headrests was classified as 'unskilled' and they earned less than male cleaners at the factory.

- They had the support of their trade union, much of the general public and the newspapers – although newspaper articles about 'plucky girls' and photographs of them having cups of tea would seem very patronising nowadays.

Finally, Barbara Castle, the Labour government's Employment Minister, was brought in to settle the dispute. The women eventually won a pay deal to put them at just over 90 per cent of the men's rate of pay for similarly skilled work.

Follow up your enquiry

Research the influence of one of the following women in working to change the role and status of women in Britain in the late 1960s and early 1970s: Barbara Castle, Shirley Williams, Vanessa Redgrave and Germaine Greer.

Source E: Women from the Dagenham Ford car factory, on strike for equal pay in London, 1968.

The 1970 Equal Pay Act

The women's strike at Dagenham and Halewood was a significant factor in bringing about the 1970 Equal Pay Act. The government was now playing a key role in legislating for change.

The 1970 Equal Pay Act was to end the inequality in wages to some extent, and it was a step in the right direction in a number of ways.

- It set out equal wages for men and women doing the same job from 1975 onwards. This was to give employers time to prepare financially for their additional staff costs.
- This legislation was also needed for Britain's entry to the **European Economic Community** (now European Union) in 1973. The British government was therefore also legislating because of pressure from Europe.

Changes by the mid-1970s

Women at work

By the mid-1970s increasing government legislation gave women more legal rights and protection both within the home and in employment. Legislation was also passed to ensure greater equality between men and women.

Activity

8. In pairs write two newspaper editorials during the time of the Ford workers' strike. One should be supporting the women's strike action and the other should be opposed to their actions.

European Economic Community: often called the 'Common Market' and now the European Union (EU), this was, and is, an organisation designed to bring European states together into a single economic market.

The main laws regarding the employment of women were:

1975 Sex Discrimination Act	Made it illegal to discriminate against women on grounds of gender in employment, education and housing.
1975 Employment Protection Act	Introduced other new important rights for working women. Pregnant women with two years' service with their employer were now entitled to six weeks' maternity pay and were entitled to keep their jobs up to 29 weeks after the birth of the child.

By the 1970s attitudes towards women working had begun to change. It was now far more socially accepted for women to return to work after having children. Women were also more likely to continue education past the compulsory school-leaving age and there was a significant increase in the proportion of female students at universities. Women were increasingly taking up careers in professions such as finance, medicine and law.

But women were still disproportionately employed in lower-paid, lower-skilled jobs and part-time employment. There were also some loopholes with the 1970 Equal Pay Act as it did not include women in jobs rarely done by men such as retail work and cleaning. Women were also underrepresented in senior management positions and were promoted much less often than men. This has sometimes been referred to as the 'glass ceiling' – meaning that there can be an upper limit to women's promotion that is not made clearly visible but which tends to prevent women being promoted beyond a certain level and achieving equality with men in the workplace.

The campaign for women's liberation did have other consequences. Many women now felt more pressurised. They increasingly felt a 'double burden' of having to prove themselves both in the workplace and in the home.

Women in politics

Women remained badly underrepresented in politics. In 1955, for example, there were only 24 female MPs out of a total of 630 in the House of Commons and after the general election in February 1974 there were 23 out of 635. In 1975, Margaret Thatcher became the first female leader of a British political party. She became leader of the Conservative Party and was to become Britain's first female Prime Minister in 1979. Margaret Thatcher was one of the few examples of a woman who was successful at this time in British national politics.

Source F: Margaret Thatcher, Conservative Party leader from 1975 and British Prime Minister from 1979 to 1990. This photograph was taken during the Conservative Party Conference in 1980.

Women in the home

Government legislation also had an impact on the status of women in the home. Two of the most significant Acts made important changes in divorce and the ownership of property by women.

Act	Before	After
1969 Divorce Reform Act	The law meant that one person had to be found guilty of committing adultery.	This Act allowed for 'no-fault' divorce following the 'irretrievable breakdown' of a marriage.
1970 Matrimonial Proceedings and Property Act	The amount of work done by women in the home was not seen as significant in divorce settlements.	This Act accepted that women's work in the home should be taken into account for a divorce settlement.

These Acts were clearly significant for women's legal rights within marriage and the home, as well as increasing equality between men and women.

The Women's Aid Federation was set up in 1974. This organisation helped to develop facilities and support for women and their children who were suffering from domestic violence. This led to issues being discussed in Parliament and in 1976 the first Domestic Violence Act was passed. This made violence against both men and women in the home a criminal offence.

What didn't change by the mid-1970s?

In some areas of society there was still very little change in attitudes towards women and sexual discrimination. For example:

- In 1970 *The Sun* newspaper used a nude model for the first time and by the mid-1970s the 'Page 3' feature had become a regular, yet controversial, feature of what had become Britain's best-selling tabloid newspaper.
- Women's magazines still focused primarily on traditional gender issues such as fashion, dieting, romance and the family.
- Children's toys in many ways reinforced gender stereotypes, as did children's reading books such as the *Janet and John* series and fiction such as *The Famous Five* stories. These were very common children's books and included stories and pictures such as boys helping dad clean and mend the car, while girls worked in the home with their mother.
- In schools, subjects such as physics, chemistry, woodwork and metalwork were still very much 'boys' subjects', while cookery and typing were very much 'girls' subjects'.

Activity

9. Using the tables on pages 23 and 24, which Act do you think was most significant in improving the role and status of women in each of the following areas?

    a) Employment.

    b) The home.

 Your conclusion so far

From this topic you have seen that:

- Changing attitudes in society and government have changed the role and status of women.
- These changes have had an effect on women's education and employment.
- These changes have affected the role of women in the home.

1. From what you have learned in this topic so far, how much changed for women in the period 1955 to 1975?

    To answer this question use a double page and give it the title: 'Change in the position of women in Britain 1955–1975'.

    Draw a line across the middle of the double page. Mark one end of the line 'Little change' and the other end 'Major change'.

- Where along the line would you place the following categories?
    - Work
    - Education
    - Home
    - Politics
    - Wages
- Write an explanation for each, giving your reason for placing the category where you have.

2. In pairs, write a conversation between a mother and her 16-year-old daughter in the mid-1950s. In the conversation the mother is offering her daughter advice about her future. Now write the same conversation between a mother and her daughter in the mid-1970s.

A3 The liberalisation of society

Learning outcomes

By the end of this topic, you should be able to:

- understand what is meant by the liberalisation of society
- describe the key changes in British society from 1955 to 1975
- evaluate the impact of these changes on family and society in Britain from 1955 to 1975.

What is the 'liberalisation of society?'

From the early 1960s until the mid-1970s the British government passed laws which covered important social issues.

These laws:

- made divorce much easier to obtain
- legalised abortion
- decriminalised homosexuality
- ended capital punishment.

Because these laws gave more rights and freedoms to individuals, this is often called the 'liberalisation of society'.

When in Britain was the 'liberalisation of society'?

Many of the laws bringing about these changes in society were passed during Harold Wilson's Labour government (1964–1970). The Labour Home Secretary, Roy Jenkins, is often seen as the key individual responsible for bringing about the significant changes regarding capital punishment and divorce, and for giving the government's support to the legalisation of abortion. Many of these laws were passed during a very brief two-year period from 1965 to 1967.

A summary of changes in British society between 1955 and 1975

1955	1975
Virtually impossible for an unmarried mother to keep a child.	Single-parent families were far more accepted.
The female contraceptive pill was not available.	The female contraceptive pill was widely available.
Capital punishment by hanging was still used for certain crimes.	Capital punishment was abolished.
It was extremely difficult to end a marriage.	Divorce was much easier to obtain and was more accepted.
Homosexuality between men was illegal and a prisonable offence.	Homosexuality between men over the age of 21 was legal.

However, even though most of the liberalising laws were passed in the mid-1960s, not all society was suddenly more liberal. People's attitudes and beliefs can take much longer to change. Some remained opposed to the 'liberalisation of society' and for many people in Britain's increasingly multicultural society, some of these changes were often in direct contrast to their deeply held religious and social beliefs.

Liberalisation: the relaxation of previous restrictions, whether by government or society in general.

Changes to the franchise

An area where the government took steps to improve individual rights and fairness within society was the age at which men and women could vote in elections. For some it seemed absurd that a 16-year-old could join the armed forces but they could not vote until the age of 21.

In 1969 the Representation of the People Act reduced the minimum voting age in Britain from 21 to 18 – although the minimum age for anyone wishing to stand as an MP still remained at 21.

Franchise: the right to vote in both local and national government elections.

The abolition of the death penalty

The first major change in the law which can be seen as part of the 'liberalisation of society' was the abolition of the death penalty. Opposition to the use of capital punishment was becoming much stronger, both in Parliament and among the general public.

In the early 1950s the average number of hangings in Britain was about 15 a year. Three notable cases – the Bentley, Ellis and Evans cases – where the death penalty was used were significant in the growth of opposition to the use of capital punishment in Britain.

Derek Bentley

In 1952 in Croydon, south London, two teenagers were involved in the shooting of a London policeman during a robbery.

The teenager who actually fired the shot was only 16 and too young to be hanged. The older boy, Derek Bentley, was 19. He suffered from learning difficulties. Despite a petition by 200 MPs, he was hanged in January 1953.

There was significant public unease that Bentley, a 19-year-old with a mental age of 11, and who had not actually fired the gun, had been hanged. This led to a widespread national debate in newspapers, on the television and radio about the use of the death penalty. Immediately after Bentley's hanging a campaign began to clear his name; this eventually led to an official government pardon in 1998.

Ruth Ellis

Another notable case was Ruth Ellis in 1955. Although she had suffered abuse from her partner, Ruth Ellis was found guilty of murdering her lover with multiple gunshots and she was sentenced to death. She was also the mother of a three-year-old child. There was widespread public and media opposition to the judge's decision. A petition of 50,000 signatures was rejected by the Conservative Home Secretary.

On the night before her hanging the governor of Holloway Prison, north London, had to call the police because of the large crowd which had gathered to protest outside the prison. She was to become the last woman to be hanged in Britain.

Timothy Evans

In 1960, Timothy Evans received a posthumous pardon. He had been hanged in 1950 for the murder of his baby daughter. Later evidence suggested that the crime had probably been committed by another man who lived in the same house and who was also responsible for other murders.

The public outcry at this miscarriage of justice played a significant part in the abolition of the death penalty in Britain.

Source A: Protestors demonstrating outside Wandsworth Prison, south London, in January 1953 against the execution of Derek

Since the Second World War there had been two attempts by the government to end the death penalty. In 1965, however, the law regarding the use of capital punishment in Britain finally changed.

A timeline showing Parliament's role in ending the death penalty in Britain

1947 and 1956	On both these occasions the House of Commons had voted to abolish the death penalty but the House of Lords rejected the change in the law.
1957	The Conservative government limited the number of cases which carried the death penalty to murders of a police or prison officer, murders caused by shooting or bombing, or murdering while being arrested.
1965	The death penalty by hanging (apart from for treason, arson in royal dockyards and violent piracy) was abolished for a trial period of five years. Life imprisonment became the alternative to hanging. This became permanent in British law in 1969.

Activities

4. Carry out a survey on attitudes to capital punishment in Britain today.

5. In pairs write two speeches as MPs in 1965. One should be a speech supporting the use of capital punishment and one should be for its abolition.

Follow up your enquiry

In groups of three carry out more detailed research about public reaction to one of the following cases:

- Timothy Evans
- Ruth Ellis
- Derek Bentley.

Attitudes towards unmarried mothers in the 1950s and 1960s

One of the most significant social changes in Britain by the 1970s was the attitude towards unmarried mothers by both the government and the general public. As part of the overall 'liberalisation of society' the situation for unmarried pregnant women changed considerably.

In the 1950s and 1960s being pregnant and unmarried was a very shameful and humiliating experience. Examples of this, and the treatment of single pregnant women, can be seen in Source B. It often remained a closely guarded family secret. To live as a single-parent mother was virtually impossible. Some women handed their child over to another married member of their family, friends or neighbours to raise as their own child.

Many unmarried pregnant women were sent away secretly by their own families to give birth in what were known as 'unmarried mothers' homes'. In the 1950s, around 200 such homes existed across Britain. Figures suggest that every year up to 40,000 unmarried pregnant women were sent to these institutions. The existence of these homes continued until the late 1960s, and almost half the pregnant women sent to these institutions were teenagers.

There was no overall government regulation of these unmarried mothers' homes so the standards of care in these homes varied tremendously:

- The majority were run by church organisations.
- Most women were pressurised to give up their child for adoption. Many were simply unaware of their rights to keep the child if they wished to do so.
- Some of these institutions had very poor standards of hygiene and food.
- The mothers were sometimes used for cheap labour.
- Many of these homes had no trained medical staff.

Source B: A woman writing in 2002 remembers her experiences of being an unmarried mother in 1957.

Run by the evangelical Mission of Hope, Birdhurst Lodge in Croydon offered temporary shelter from a bleak postwar world where unmarried women who got pregnant out of wedlock – even in cases of rape – were considered little better than prostitutes. They were often spirited off to brutal 'unmarried mothers' homes', and there, in those days before IVF, when many infertile couples were desperate to adopt, they could find themselves pressed relentlessly to give up their child…[Some homes] were run by nuns who referred to their charges as 'fallen women' and would hand babies over to wealthy couples in exchange for a handsome 'donation' to the convent. The nuns would then put the anguished mothers to work as 'lifers' in the laundry, unless a relative agreed to come and collect them…The only cases that [a woman employed in the home] can recall of a mother keeping her baby without a struggle tended to be ones where the child was born disabled. In such cases, nobody rushed to adopt the child. Mothers were even encouraged to buy a pack of baby clothes to hand over to the adoptive parents of their child…State support was also so meagre [small] that most single mothers could only realistically afford to keep their babies if the extended family came to the rescue, quietly absorbing an extra child…Greedier homes deliberately split twins up to get two 'donations', often never even telling adoptive parents that their new baby had been one of a pair.

M. Paton, *The Guardian*, 31'10'2007. Copyright Guardian News & Media Ltd 2007.

Activities

6. In groups, write four diary entries to show the situation of an unmarried mother who enters a home and gives up her baby for adoption. Date the entries at:
   - five months' pregnant
   - eight months' pregnant
   - one week after the birth
   - one month after the birth.

   Make sure you include the attitudes of her parents and the people in the home, and whether she meets the people who adopt her baby.

7. What can you learn from Source B about:
   - attitudes to unmarried mothers in Britain in the late 1950s?
   - the treatment of unmarried mothers in Britain in the 1950s?

Source C: An unmarried mother caring for her baby in an unmarried mothers' home in 1962, run by the London Diocesan Council for Moral Welfare.

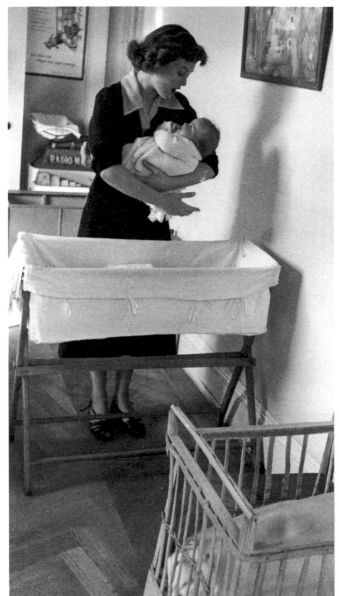

Abortion

Rather than the stigma of being an unmarried mother another 'choice' available to women was to terminate their pregnancy illegally. Before 1967, abortion was illegal in Britain except in a few cases that were performed for strictly medical reasons when the mother's health was seen to be seriously at risk. The legalisation of abortion in Britain was probably one of the most controversial laws passed in the 1960s. In fact, the legalisation of abortion was not seen by the government as part of liberalising society but more as a response to concerns about public health.

Poorer women were often forced to resort to what were commonly known as 'backstreet abortions'. Backstreet abortions used a variety of dangerous methods to try to terminate unwanted pregnancies. Methods used included the use of chemicals, pumps, alcohol, knitting needles, and coat-hangers. One of the most dangerous methods used a lead-based liquid which poisoned many women.

Obviously, there are no official statistics on the number of backstreet abortions that took place, though there are some estimates that up to 20,000 were performed in Britain each year. There are, however, official NHS records. These figures show that, before the legalisation of abortion, the NHS treated 35,000 women for attempted abortions that led to medical problems in the period 1948–1967. Some women suffered permanent health damage or even died as a result of having a backstreet abortion.

Some wealthier women were able to use private clinics. These clinics were strictly illegal and provided a lucrative income for some doctors. Some historians estimate that in the early 1960s over 10,000 private abortions took place every year in central London alone for those women who could afford it.

This combination of the very real health dangers to many pregnant women, as well as the profiteering by some doctors performing illegal abortions, encouraged some MPs to support the legalisation of abortion.

Follow up your enquiry

Go to www.pearsonhotlinks.co.uk, insert express code 6442P and follow the link to watch 'Shooting People: A World without Abortion' – a short video clip in which a British woman talks of her moving experiences in early 1960s Britain. What can you learn from this woman's own experiences about attitudes to abortion in Britain during the 1960s?

The legalisation of abortion

Before the Second World War, the Abortion Law Reform Association had been set up. This movement grew during the 1950s, but with a very small membership of just over 1,000 members it did not have very much influence.

A major factor which led to the growth of support for the legalisation of abortion were the extremely severe side-effects of the so-called wonder-drug thalidomide.

Thalidomide was a drug that could prevent women suffering from morning sickness during pregnancy. It was first licensed for use in Britain in 1958 but was quickly withdrawn in 1962. The drug had led to significant numbers of seriously deformed children being born – some of whom had missing limbs. Furthermore, nearly half those children born to mothers who had used thalidomide died before their first birthday. This provided a strong argument for those campaigning for the legalisation of abortion so that the births of severely deformed babies could be prevented.

Four times since the Second World War, bills to legalise abortion (1953, 1961, 1965 and 1966) had failed to pass through Parliament. These attempts had been met with strong opposition from both the Catholic Church and from within Parliament. In 1967 David Steel, a Liberal MP, introduced a **Private Member's Bill** into the House of Commons, but he did have the Labour government's support. From the government's point of view the main reason to legalise abortion was on health grounds – to end the dangerous use of backstreet abortions. Others supporting the abortion law claimed that it would reduce:

- the number of children in care
- the number of cases of cruelty to children
- the number of illegitimate births.

There was a heated debate in the House of Commons, but the Bill was passed.

The Abortion Act 1967 legalised the termination of pregnancy up to 28 weeks if either:

- two doctors agreed that the mother's physical or mental health was at risk
- the child was likely to be born with serious mental or physical disabilities.

In the mid-1960s most medical opinion agreed that 28 weeks was the minimum time when a prematurely born baby might still survive. This time limit has since been reduced due to medical advances.

The number of legal abortions in Britain rose dramatically from 35,000 a year in 1968 to over 140,000 in 1975. This sharp rise shocked many. David Steel admitted that he had no idea at all when passing the 1967 Abortion Act that the annual rate of abortions would increase so rapidly.

Many saw the legalisation of abortion as a fundamental legal right for women to have the 'right to choose' and a vital step forward for personal freedom. Opponents saw it as a 'murderous act' which went against their religious and moral beliefs. Opposition from the Church of England and especially the Catholic Church to abortion became the basis for a wider 'Pro-Life' campaign. As well as those who argued from a religious standpoint, there were others who felt very strongly about the rights of the unborn child. Some were also concerned that, later on in life, many women might regret their decision to have had an abortion.

Private Member's Bill: proposed laws introduced by individual MPs rather than the government.

ResultsPlus
Top Tip

Do not describe the legislation of abortion as if most people suddenly accepted the change. Many remained opposed to its legalisation.

Source D: A demonstration for the legalisation of abortion outside the Houses of Parliament in 1966.

Activity

8. Make an annotated diagram to show how the following factors interacted to bring about the Abortion Act in 1967.

   - public opinion
   - the government
   - the Abortion Law Reform Association
   - key individuals (David Steel)
   - thalidomide.

ResultsPlus

Top Tip

Remember to try to show how various factors linked together to bring about the legalisation of abortion.

Preventing unwanted pregnancies

As well as legalising abortion, the government also tried other ways to prevent unwanted pregnancies. One was by gradually increasing the availability of the female contraceptive pill and the other was providing more sexual information and advice.

Condoms were relatively inexpensive and easily available from chemists and barbers but many men were not prepared to use them. A form of contraception controlled by women – the female contraceptive pill – became available on prescription to married women in 1961. Its availability as a prescribed drug on the NHS was opposed by many MPs, but MPs supporting the availability of female contraception believed it would significantly reduce the number of abortions. The Secretary of State for Social Services, Keith Joseph, regarded its main aim as being to reduce poverty by ending unwanted pregnancies.

However, its use did not soon become widespread for a number of reasons.

- It had already been used in the USA, but there were widespread concerns and health warnings about possible side effects, which included the risk of cancer.
- Some doctors resisted prescribing 'the pill' to women for moral reasons.
- The Catholic Church in Britain officially forbade its use.
- It was not available to unmarried women until 1967.

These various factors combined so that by 1970 only 20 per cent of married women and less than 10 per cent of unmarried women were using 'the pill'.

Many people believed that by making sex education more available, the number of abortions performed in Britain would be significantly reduced. In the late 1960s the government took active steps to educate and inform people more about sex.

- From 1967 onwards, the Family Planning Act meant that local health authorities were able to provide family planning advice and contraceptives.
- In the 1950s and 1960s, sex education lessons normally focused on the biological aspects of reproduction. From the early 1970s onwards, schools began to include more teaching about areas such as contraception and sexually transmitted infections.

Source E: A poster from the Family Planning Association in the early 1970s.

Would you be more careful if it was you that got pregnant?

Anyone married or single can get advice on contraception from the Family Planning Association. Margaret Pyke House, 27-35 Mortimer Street, London W1 N 8BQ. Tel. 01-636 9135.

The Health Education Council

Activities

9. In groups of four create a conversation between the following people discussing the contraceptive pill in the mid-1960s:
   - a Catholic priest
   - a married woman who does not want more children
   - a young single woman
   - a young single man.
10. What do you think is the message of Source E on pregnancy and contraception in Britain in the early 1970s?
11. 'The impact of the pill on women's lives by 1970 can easily be overestimated.' Do you agree? Explain your answer.

Changes to family life

By the mid-1970s, changes in attitudes meant that more unmarried women were able to live as single-parent mothers. The number of single-parent families also increased with changes to divorce laws and there was much more acceptance of single-parent families.

Before the 1960s divorce was only permitted where one person had been found guilty of adultery. It was often very difficult for this to be proved. Those wanting such evidence for a divorce, and who could afford it, often resorted to hiring private detectives. Divorce could then only be granted by the courts.

The Divorce Reform Act 1969 allowed divorce for the 'irretrievable breakdown' of a marriage. This meant a divorce could be granted if:

- the couple had spent two years living apart and both wanted to end the marriage
- the couple had spent five years living apart and one wanted to end the marriage.

This led to a significant increase in the number of divorces. By the mid-1970s, the number of divorces every year was about one third of the number of marriages.

Homosexuality

In the late 1950s a series of well-known public figures had been convicted and imprisoned for homosexuality. A report published by Lord Wolfenden in 1957 recommended the decriminalisation of male homosexuality for men aged 21 and over. This was met with a fierce debate within government and among the general public. It was not until a decade later that the 1967 Sexual Offences Act **decriminalised** homosexuality for men aged 21 and over (except for those serving in the armed forces, and it did not include Northern Ireland). The main reason for the legislation was not to endorse homosexuality, but to prevent homosexual men from being blackmailed rather than risk imprisonment.

The combination of all these factors added up to what is often called a 'sexual revolution' during the 1960s.

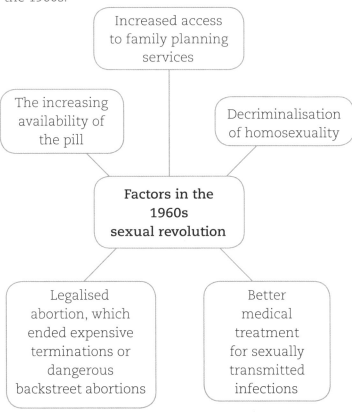

Activities

12. Why had family life in Britain changed so much by the mid-1970s?
13. 'During the 1960s, Britain experienced a "sexual revolution".' Do you agree? Explain your answer.

Decriminalisation: legislation that makes something legal that was formerly illegal.

Follow up your enquiry

Mary Whitehouse and Barbara Castle were two prominent women in the 1960s. Research their roles and attitudes towards changes in British society in the 1960s.

The effects of the 'liberalisation of society'

In many ways, from the late 1960s various laws gradually combined to change people's attitudes towards a whole range of issues such as the death penalty, marriage, the family and sex.

On the one hand, the 'liberalisation of society' can be seen as a move towards a more humane society. Supporters of these changes would argue that they allowed for more individual freedom and increasing personal happiness. The changes meant less control by the state over individuals' personal lives and changing attitudes meant less personal restraint.

Others see such changes as being responsible for a rise in social problems. The 'liberalisation of society' is seen by some as being responsible for a decline in moral values and standards of behaviour.

Activity

14. A survey carried out in Britain in 1969 on which changes during the 1960s people agreed with the most showed:

- 5 per cent supported the new laws on abortion, divorce and homosexuality.
- 70 per cent agreed that 'murderers should be hanged'.

What do these figures suggest to you about how much public attitudes had really changed?

Activities

15. Look at the factors below. Sort them into: a) arguments supporting the 'liberalisation of society' and b) arguments opposing the 'liberalisation of society':
- rising number of abortions
- more pressure to have sex
- women having the freedom to choose when to have children
- the right to end an unhappy marriage
- less commitment to marriage
- the need for a 'traditional family'.

16. Which of the laws passed for 'the liberalisation of society' do you think a) the government and b) the public would most likely want to change back?

17. In pairs, write two speeches. One should argue that the government was responsible for the 'liberalisation of society' and the other that the public was more responsible.

 Your conclusion so far

From this topic we have seen that:

- Changing attitudes in society and the actions taken by governments have changed the way in which many people now lead their lives.
- These changes have included the ending of capital punishment, the availability of more forms of contraception and safe legalised abortion, the ability to divorce, and the legalisation of homosexuality.

From what you have learned in this topic so far, how much changed in British society during the period 1955 to 1975?

To answer this question:

- explain the way many British people lived in the 1950s
- identify changes by the mid-1970s
- explain why some people supported and some opposed these changes
- decide how much change there was in the years 1955–1975 in social attitudes and in the way people could behave.

A4 The swinging sixties?

Learning outcomes

By the end of this topic, you should be able to:

- define what is meant by 'swinging sixties'
- understand how society changed during the sixties
- explain the ways in which the sixties could be described as 'swinging'.

Revolution!

As you have seen, there were major changes in society during this period:

- Immigrants arrived from Commonwealth countries.
- Attitudes towards women changed.
- Changes were made in the law, reflecting different attitudes on a range of issues such as the vote, the death penalty and sex.

The changing role of young people in society

1945: the end of the Second World War

Teenagers and young people who lived at home had more money to spend on themselves.

Changes during the 1950s
- Changes in education
- Improved employment opportunities and pay
- Changes in technology

Young adults were more likely to move away from home to study at university or to work in towns.

Fashion and design

Pop culture

The influence of teenagers on sixties society

Challenges to authority and tradition

No one is sure exactly how this period became known as the 'swinging sixties' but 'swinging', 'with it', 'mod' and 'groovy' were all phrases used to describe something in the latest fashion. It is possible the term 'swinging sixties' came from 1966, when the American magazine *Time* ran a front cover with the heading 'London: The Swinging City' showing images of fashion, music and the 'London scene'.

The birth of the 'teenager'

For many people there was a sense of living in a new era during the sixties. This was particularly true of youth and young adults. Before the Second World War (1939–1945) many young people would leave school and start work at the age of 14. They would be treated as adults and their lives would be very similar to those of their parents. After the war life began to change.

'Teenagers' were a new section of society, with their own interests and attitudes. Different sets began to define themselves through clothes and music, for example:

- Modern youth, or 'mods', rode mopeds, wore tailored clothes and aimed for a clean and sophisticated image; they listened to rhythm and blues or ska music.
- The American-influenced 'rockers' rode motor bikes, wore leather jackets and preferred rock and roll music.

This sense of identity was also developed by magazines such as *Honey* (first published in 1960). They were aimed at teenagers and included news about fashion and music, advice and advertisements on make-up and photographs of celebrities.

The new **youth culture** encouraged young people to expect a good social life. According to research by Mark Abrams published in *The Teenage Consumer* in 1959 and 1961 – teenagers bought 33 per cent of cinema tickets, 33 per cent of cosmetics and 40 per cent of music records.

The feeling developed that there was something special about youth culture during the sixties and it is true that models like Twiggy, musicians such as

The Beatles, designers like Mary Quant, and writers such as Alan Bennett were then aged between 17 and 25. Many film stars, writers and people in the entertainment industry wanted to associate themselves with this new youth culture.

Meanwhile, groups of young people questioned the older generation's emphasis on duty and self-discipline. They felt entitled to enjoy themselves, to express their opinions and to try new experiences. Rebellion against the older generation's values also became easier when teenagers had their own money to buy the shocking clothes and music that were fashionable.

A small group of people, based in London, were seen as trendsetters. These included Mary Quant and Barbara Hulanicki, the models Twiggy and Jean Shrimpton (all important fashion **icons**), the actor Terence Stamp, and the photographer David Bailey. They were often photographed and their activities were widely reported.

Activities

1. Make a list of the things you spend your spare money on each week and rank it in order of importance to you.

2. If your parents made a list of how they spent their spare money, how similar would it be to yours?

3. To what extent do you think young people nowadays aim to rebel and shock through the way they dress or the music they listen to?

4. Explain which of the following you feel was the most important factor in creating a new youth culture during the sixties:

    a) increased wealth of young people

    b) new independent attitudes

    c) trendsetting individuals

    d) magazines which publicised new trends.

Youth culture: the fashions and trends popular among young people.

Icon: something which sums up the mood of the time; it can be used as a symbol for the period.

Icons of the sixties: the mini

Source A: An extract from *Mary Quant's Mini Skirt: a Mini History*, from a website about women's fashion.

> Before the 1960s there was little to no fashion created specifically for teenage youth – only children's wear and adults' fashion. This was before the iconic Mary Quant opened 'Bazaar', one of the first boutiques of its kind. 'Bazaar' was entirely dedicated to teenage youth, filled with skinny-rib jumpers, knee high boots, white detachable collars, and – of course – the legendary mini skirt… Since about 1958, skirts have become progressively shorter, and although Quant didn't essentially invent the mini skirt she was nevertheless the first to design and market it successfully to the younger market. Mary Quant saw the mini to be both liberating and practical, and therefore particularly relevant to teenage youth in her era.

Source B: The story of the mini car – an extract from the website, *Icons: a portrait of England*.

> The Mini…was to be the smallest car BMC produced…The Mini Cooper was launched in 1961. It was designed…for the racing circuits…and went racing in the Monte Carlo rally every year, winning the event no fewer than three times…In the early 1960s, the Mini began to acquire a layer of cool. All four members of the Beatles bought one, as did a string of movie stars – from Steve McQueen to Brigitte Bardot. Racing-drivers were seen driving them. Even the Queen owned a Mini.

Fashions of the sixties

Some of the fashion styles of the sixties, including mods, rockers, beatniks, hippies and skinheads.

Activities

5. Explain how both the mini skirt and the mini car symbolised ideas of freedom and independence.
6. How much do you think the mini skirt and car actually affected the lives people led?

Fashion

During the sixties, there was a reaction against the smart dress code of the older generation. Fewer women wore hats and gloves, fewer men wore business suits. There was less emphasis on different clothes for daytime and evening. Women wore trousers more often and some clothes were deliberately 'unisex'. Tights allowed women more freedom in dress than stockings had done, but it also became acceptable to have bare legs, and to have hair loose rather than coiled smoothly. In fact there were many different trends in fashion during the sixties:

- bold, primary colours and geometric patterns but also pastel colours, flowery and swirling patterns, lace and ruffles
- sharply tailored suits, simple shapes such as the mini skirt and pinafore but also the hippy style of long, flowing skirts
- natural materials such as cotton, silk and velvet were used but so were nylon and plastic.

Fashions changed quickly and clothes were produced cheaply, in the expectation that they would only be worn for a limited period.

Activities

7. Research art and design during this period and explain how it fits in with the idea of the 'swinging sixties', for example the work of artists David Hockney and Bridget Riley, and the designs of Terence Conran (who set up Habitat).

8. In groups, research the fashion styles of mods, rockers, beatniks, hippies, skinheads and punks. One person from each group should present their findings to the rest of the class and then have a class vote to decide which trend most people prefer.

9. Use the research to create a poster montage or PowerPoint® presentation summing up the various fashion styles and the key influences on mainstream fashion; make sure you include:

   a) Mary Quant, the designer

   b) Laura Ashley, the designer

   c) Barbara Hulanicki, who set up the Biba boutique

   d) The Beatles

   e) a fashion magazine such as *Honey*

   f) Vidal Sassoon, the hairdresser

   g) Diana Rigg in *The Avengers* television programme

   h) psychedelia.

10. In what ways were these fashions more suited to young people than to the older generation?

11. How would a historian decide which fashion style was 'typical' of the sixties' period?

12. Copy and complete the diagram below. Provide an example of each of the factors

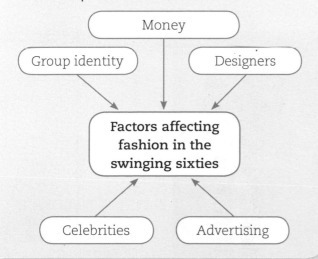

Source C: A photograph of Carnaby Street, in London in 1968 – seen around the world as one of the main fashion centres in 'swinging London'.

Twist and shout

Music was an important way for different groups of young people to establish an identity but it also had an enormous influence on the ideas and attitudes of the new youth culture. For the first time, most groups were writing their own songs and many of the lyrics reflected key ideas of love, freedom, and happiness.

The 'Beat Generation' in the USA during the fifties had been a form of rebellion – beatniks wanted freedom to live in a different way. They often discussed ideas about life and held gatherings where they read poetry, studied abstract art and listened to jazz music or bongo drums. These 'hip' ideas spread to Britain during the fifties and early sixties.

British singers were also heavily influenced by American rock and roll music, especially Bill Hayley and the Comets, and Elvis Presley. However, British songwriters developed their own brands of music and a number of different styles evolved.

Young people now had the spare cash to buy records regularly and portable record players meant that groups often gathered to listen to their choice of music away from older people. This became a common way for young people to spend their free time and was a major factor in the development of pop culture.

Source D:
A portable record player from the 1960s (but it still needed to be plugged into an electricity supply).

New technology also led to the mass production of transistor radios. They were cheap, and they did not need to be plugged in, meaning that for the first time, young people could take their music with them wherever they went.

Did you know?

'Pirate' radio

The BBC was the only legal radio station but an illegal station, called Radio Caroline, began to broadcast in 1964. It operated from a ship which was anchored just off the Suffolk coast. It was in international waters and so was not affected by British regulations. A number of similar 'pirate' radio stations were set up during the sixties and many young people enjoyed the feeling of rebellion that they gained from listening to these stations in secret.

In 1967 BBC Radio 1 started to broadcast 'popular' music, trying to reach the same groups who were already listening to **'pirate' radio** stations like Radio Caroline.

Television was also an important way of spreading youth culture. *Juke Box Jury* and *Thank Your Lucky Stars* asked a panel to rate new songs while programmes like *Top of the Pops* showed fashionably dressed crowds dancing to the music being played in the studio. 'The weekend starts here!' was the catchphrase of *Ready, Steady, Go!* and Cathy McGowan, one of the show's presenters, also became a style icon.

Pop culture

The Beatles were particularly influential and although their music was usually about 'boy meets girl' romance, a number of their songs contained reflections on different problems in society, such as *Eleanor Rigby* and *She's Leaving Home*. The BBC banned the song *Lucy in the Sky with Diamonds*, which was on the 1967 album *Sergeant Pepper's Lonely Hearts Club Band*, because it was believed to be a reference to the drug LSD. In 1967 The Beatles also became involved with the Indian religious leader, Maharishi Mahesh Yogi and their music reflected this new influence using Indian instruments. In 1970, The Beatles announced their breakup but all four members then had successful solo careers.

For many people, they typify sixties music as they went from early songs about love to more experimental music and lyrics. In 1964, they made their first film and in 1965, they were awarded the MBE (a highly prestigious award).

Source E: The Beatles at the time of the *Sergeant Pepper's Lonely Hearts Club Band* album.

Source F: A photograph of The Rolling Stones in the sixties.

In contrast to The Beatles, The Rolling Stones and The Who created a much more energetic sound and had a more rebellious attitude. They developed a reputation for bad behaviour, such as swearing on stage, smashing up instruments, using drugs and having casual sex.

By 1975, the punk movement was emerging and took this rebellious aggression even further in both fashion and music, expressed through ripped clothes, use of safety pins, brightly dyed and lacquered hair styles, and anti-establishment music like *Anarchy in the UK*, which was released by the Sex Pistols in 1976.

Nevertheless, throughout the sixties and into the seventies, traditional artists continued to be successful, singing ballads and more conventional songs. Artists such as The Beatles got a lot of publicity because some young women screamed and became hysterical but the biggest-selling single of 1965 was in fact *Tears* by Ken Dodd, showing the continuing popularity of more conventional music.

Films and television

British films won a number of Oscars during the sixties and featured major stars like Richard Burton and Peter O'Toole. This contributed to the feeling that Britain was successful and a world leader in culture.

Programmes on television included *The Avengers*, *Come Dancing*, *The Benny Hill Show*, *Coronation Street*, *Love Thy Neighbour*, and *Top of the Pops*. The range of programmes reflects both the traditional types of information and entertainment, and the new attitudes to female equality, racial integration, and a belief in progress.

However, television also had a big effect on society through programmes like *Cathy Come Home*, screened in 1966, which was about the problems of poverty.

Activities

13. Draw a topic web to show how music influenced youth culture. Make sure you include an explanation of the links to magazines, television and fashion.

14. In small groups, discuss how far the behaviour of famous musicians influences our attitudes nowadays to issues such as casual sex, drugs, alcohol and homosexuality.

Follow up your enquiry

The Beatles and The Rolling Stones were two major pop bands during the sixties but they are also remembered because they went on for many years afterwards. Other groups were also very important at the time but receive less attention because they disbanded and their music is less likely to be played now. Go to www. pearsonhotlinks.co.uk and enter express code 6442P. Find out more about music in the sixties and then create a fact file using the information you have found.

Activities

15. Why do you think the BBC provided relatively few programmes aimed at young adults when the music and fashion industries were so quick to adapt to the new youth culture?

16. How important do you think radio, television and magazines were in spreading the youth culture that was developing in cities such as London, Liverpool, Manchester to the rest of Britain?

17. Find out about the way the problems of the sixties were shown in *Cathy Come Home*, *Up the Junction* and *A Taste of Honey*.

Challenges to tradition and authority

Some women saw the contraceptive pill and the legalisation of abortion as freeing them from the traditional roles of wife and mother. Changed attitudes towards sex and homosexuality were another way of rebelling against 'old fashioned' ideas. Meanwhile, the hippies spread their message of flower power and free love by rejecting traditional values and wealth and 'dropping out' of society.

Other young people became concerned about **apartheid** in South Africa, the role of the USA in Vietnam and the threat of nuclear war. There were protest rallies and marches, and student groups, in particular, were very critical of the government.

> **Apartheid:** separateness of races – a system of racial segregation used in South Africa between 1948 and 1993.

Source G: Police and protesters clash at Grosvenor Square, London on March 17 1968.

Source H: A description, written by an eyewitness, in *The Guardian* newspaper, of a 1968 protest that ended in violent scenes outside the American embassy in Grosvenor Square, London.

> On March 17 1968, there was a big anti-Vietnam war rally in Trafalgar Square in London. Afterwards, 8,000 mainly youthful protesters marched on Grosvenor Square, where a letter of protest was delivered to the American embassy. The crowd, though, refused to disperse, and a fierce battle ensued between demonstrators and riot police. Protesters hurled mud, stones, firecrackers and smoke bombs; mounted police responded with charges. The violence of the struggle, in the cosseted heart of Mayfair, shocked everyone. By the end of the afternoon, more than 200 people had been arrested.

J. Henley, *The Guardian*, 21/05/2008. Copyright Guardian News & Media Ltd 2008.

The idea that traditional society could be challenged was also reinforced by a new BBC programme, *That Was The Week That Was*, broadcast from 1962 to 1963, which poked fun at the establishment – the traditional sources of power and control in the country.

Violence and rebellion

Mods and rockers clashed on a number of occasions but the most famous was on May bank holiday in 1964, which became known as the 'Battle of Brighton'.

Source I: An extract from *The Encyclopaedia of Brighton* by Tim Carder, published in 1990, describes the violence at Brighton.

> The town was invaded by up to 3,000 youths. The leather-jacketed 'Rockers' arrived on their motor-bikes on the Sunday morning, but were challenged in the afternoon by a much larger number of the neatly-dressed 'Mods' on their motor-scooters. Several small scuffles broke out, but the most serious trouble was around the Palace Pier where hundreds of deckchairs were broken, pebbles were used as missiles, and the Savoy Cinema windows were smashed. Eventually 150 police and a police horse quelled the disturbance, but the violence was repeated the following morning with several thousand spectators watching the confrontations.

Although violence did not happen regularly on a large scale, it was widely publicised, reinforcing the image of a rebellious and aggressive youth culture.

This image of youth was made worse in the mid-sixties, when football hooliganism became a concern. Groups of youths known as 'skinheads' were also often associated with violence.

Activities

18. Discuss which aspect of youth culture – the 'flower power and free love' movement, protest marches and rallies, or the use of violence:

    a) is most typical of young people's attitudes during the sixties

    b) posed the greatest threat to authority at the time.

19. Working in groups and using the information in the earlier sections of this book as well as this chapter, write a discussion between the following characters about life in Britain during the sixties:

    a) a West Indian immigrant

    b) a policeman

    c) a young woman living in London

    d) a parent worried about their teenage child.

    Make sure the discussion covers issues such as racial tensions, violence, fashion or music, and changing attitudes towards women or sex.

Reviewing the sixties

The emphasis on youth culture makes the sixties seem to be focused on fashion, music and fun. However, this period is also associated with ideas such as freedom, independence, tolerance of other ideas on sex, and rebellion against established and traditional views.

Follow up your enquiry

Find out about the Profumo scandal or the trial of Penguin publishers in 1960 (for publishing *Lady Chatterley's Lover* by D. H. Lawrence) and explain how the example you have chosen might have affected attitudes towards authority.

Source J: A photograph of violence during the 'Battle of Brighton' in 1964.

 Your conclusion so far

From this topic we have seen the 'swinging sixties' is a term used to describe youth culture during the 1960s. It has strong associations with:

- the music of The Beatles
- fashion such as the mini skirt
- leisure and entertainment.

From what you have learned in this topic so far, explain why you think the sixties was called 'swinging'. To answer this question you will need to explain:

- why there seemed to be a new sense of freedom, independence and toleration in fashion and music
- how young people developed a sense of identity
- how attitudes towards women changed
- why London and other major cities became centres of this new culture.

Enquiry and writing skills support

Learning outcomes

By the end of this section, you should be able to:

*   follow up an enquiry
*   select and organise your material
*   write up your enquiry.

In this section we will see how to complete the stages of following up an enquiry. The diagram on this page shows you the enquiry stages and what you need to do.

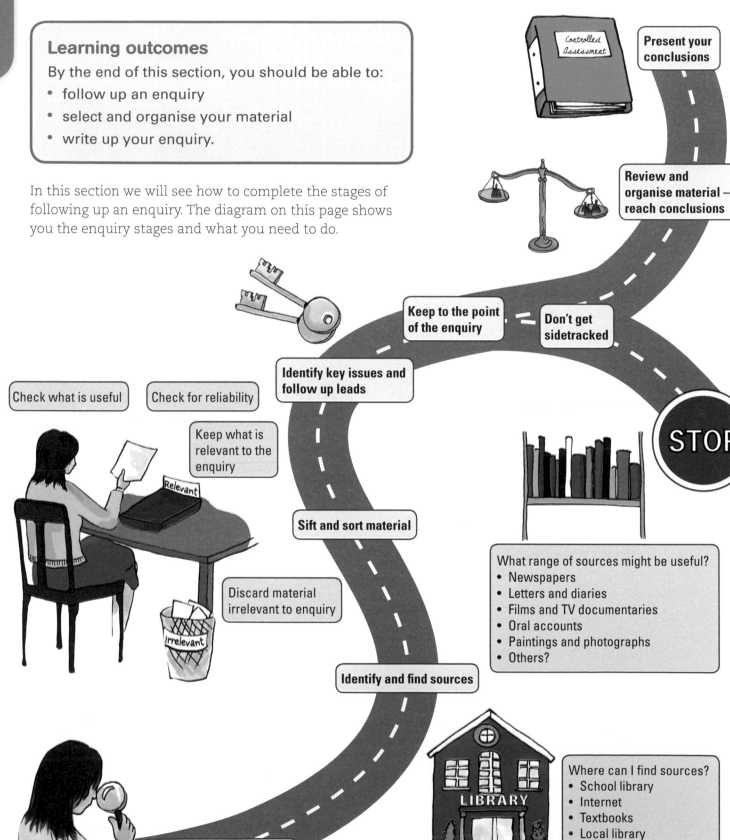

Present your conclusions

Review and organise material – reach conclusions

Keep to the point of the enquiry

Don't get sidetracked

Identify key issues and follow up leads

Check what is useful

Check for reliability

Keep what is relevant to the enquiry

Relevant

STOP

Sift and sort material

What range of sources might be useful?
*   Newspapers
*   Letters and diaries
*   Films and TV documentaries
*   Oral accounts
*   Paintings and photographs
*   Others?

Discard material irrelevant to enquiry

Irrelevant

Identify and find sources

Where can I find sources?
*   School library
*   Internet
*   Textbooks
*   Local library
*   Others?

What is the enquiry about?

Following up an enquiry 1: The reasons for the Notting Hill riots in 1958

Your controlled assessment Part A task will be similar to this one:

> **Enquiry focus**
>
> Your enquiry task will focus on the reasons for the 1958 Notting Hill race riots against the background of post-war immigration to Britain.

In this practice example we are going to follow up the enquiry focus. You will be able to use the skills you develop to follow up your own Part A enquiry.

What is this enquiry about?

Your first step is to identify the precise enquiry. In this instance, it's about the reasons behind the Notting Hill riots. You need to think about what caused the riots in this part of London in 1958, as well as the long-term background of problems facing immigrants to Britain after the Second World War.

Identify and find sources

The next stage is to gather your information. Start with an easy outline book and read through the relevant material. Write some summary notes, making sure you include the book title, author and the pages where you have found the information. You should only start to look for more in-depth information when you have used two or three textbooks which give you the basic information.

For this enquiry, begin by re-reading pages 4–14 of this book and completing the activities on this page.

To add to your sources, you might start by doing a quick search on the internet but you should also look at books by historians. When you find a book, check the book contents page and the index to make sure it covers the topic you want to research. For this enquiry, look up 'immigration', 'Notting Hill' and 'race riots'. You could also use television documentaries as a source of information but be careful to check them against other sources to be sure they have not been too dramatised or exaggerated.

Sift and sort material

Go through your new sources and make additional notes. It will help if you use a fresh page for each book or other source of information. Remember that the book or the webpage you've found was not written to answer your specific question! For example, this enquiry is about the events leading to the Notting Hill riots in 1958. You have to choose what to take from your source to answer that – see the activities on page 46.

Look for new leads to follow up. For example, if a source tells you that 'a culture of drinking places, ska music and blues clubs' was developing and that 'Teddy Boys were beginning to attack black immigrants' this means it added to the tension in different ways:

- Immigrants often had a different culture to that of the white population.
- Teenage groups were attacking immigrants.

Activities

Making notes

1. Make a bullet point list of useful information from your first source of information about the experience of immigrants in Britain in the 1950s and why this may have led to the Notting Hill riots in 1958. For example:
    - They were often well qualified but found it hard to get good jobs.
    - Trade unions complained they took jobs for less pay.
2. Now repeat this process for two other textbooks or simple overviews.
3. Begin to organise your notes. You could sort them into a chart like the one below.

The problems facing immigrants in Britain in the 1950s	The responses by the British public to immigration in the 1950s
Hard to find accommodation	There were signs: 'Keep Britain White'
Hard to find jobs	

Make each of your points a separate row in the chart.

You could follow up these two leads, going through the same process of finding, sifting and sorting and noting information.

ResultsPlus

Top Tip

Looking for information can be a slow process. You might read through a lot to get a small piece of new information. But your work is better if you concentrate on what's new and relevant, rather than adding something that repeats information you already have or is not relevant.

Stick to the enquiry path

Don't go off track! On a journey, detours and side roads can be great fun and you can follow them up just because they are interesting. Remember, though, to return to your enquiry path – and not to add in material which isn't relevant. For example information about the effects of the Race Relations Act wouldn't help you answer an enquiry about the reasons for the Notting Hill riots in 1958.

Source A: An extract from *OCR GCSE Modern World History,* by Ben Walsh, published in 2009.

> In the later 1950s some right-wing activists began a campaign to 'keep Britain white'. The former Fascist leader, Oswald Mosley, saw an opportunity to make use of the ill feeling towards immigrants and place himself at the head of a protest movement. He set up an organisation called the Union Movement and published anti-immigrant posters and leaflets. He was not the only person saying these things. George Rogers, the Labour MP for North Kensington, urged the government to limit the influx of immigrants into overcrowded areas and claimed that they had a particular taste for crime, drugs and knives. Comments like these increased tensions, especially since Britain's economy was beginning to take a downturn in 1958 and there was greater competition for jobs.

Using sources carefully

So far we have applied two tests when using sources – relevance and duplication. Sometimes you will also need to think about reliability. You need to be particularly careful about internet sources because they are sometimes anonymous and it is difficult to check the information they contain. Remember that many internet sites are just opinions without any factual support. You also need to think about their purpose and possible bias. As you use your sources, apply the RDR tests: **R**elevance, **D**uplication and **R**eliability.

Activities

Selecting information

4. Read Source A and decide with a partner how much of it is useful for the enquiry. Remember:

- you want to find out why the riots took place in Notting Hill in 1958

- usually you only want new points

- sometimes you may want to make a note that two sources agree about an important point.

5. Photocopy or write out the whole passage. Colour-code it: yellow for new reasons, green for information which is new and blue for repeated information. Some parts have been done for you.

Activities

Relevance and reliability

6. Study Source B. It is from an interview with a man who had recently migrated to Britain from the Caribbean.

7. Decide with a partner which of these statements you agree with. Choose as many as you like but be prepared to justify your choice.

   - It is not biased.
   - It is biased but still has some useful information.
   - It makes statements about why the Notting Hill riots took place.
   - It makes statements about the experiences faced by immigrants in post-war Britain.
   - It is mainly relevant to this enquiry.
   - It is does not add much to this enquiry.

8. Add any useful information to your notes.

Source B: From an interview with Loftus Burton after the Notting Hill riots, recorded in *1958 Remembered – Riot Reminiscence* on the website of the Kensington and Chelsea Community History Group – *History Talk*.

> The whole thing exploded in '58. It just became part of your life. I don't think it was a case of you try to forget it, blank it out of your mind, in a way you became immune to it, immune is the wrong word, it just became part and parcel of life, if you were to target all the incidents, racism that you encountered one could go on for weeks.

Identify key issues and follow up leads

So far this enquiry has provided the following leads. The words in bold could be used as headings.

- The **problems faced by immigrants** such as housing, employment and racism.
- The **influence of key individuals** such as Oswald Mosley and George Rogers, MP.
- The **role of youth groups** such as Teddy Boys.
- The **different culture** of immigrant groups.

Activities

9. Study Source C in the source file (page 48). It gives a new lead from the work of a **Black Power** activist.

10. Add information from Source C to your notes. In your real enquiry, it will help if you add page numbers, in case you want to find the passage again.

11. Begin to organise your information under key headings whenever you use a new source.

Black Power: a political slogan and a movement of people of Black African descent that grew out of the civil rights movement in America in the 1960s and 1970s. While it sought political and social equality it also emphasised racial pride in black culture and identity.

Source file

Source C: Michael de Freitas, a Black Power activist also known as Michael X, who was present at the Notting Hill riots, was quoted in *History Talk Community History Newsletter*, Issue 11, May 2008.

> The thing about the so called Notting Hill race riots is that they were not real race riots at all. People are always fighting in an area like the ghetto; clubs are always being invaded and broken up. The general opinion was that a few Teddy Boys had simply been making a nuisance of themselves.

Source D: An extract from *OCR GCSE Modern World History*, by A. Brodkin *et al*, published in 2009.

> On arrival, immigrants usually settled in a relatively small number of towns and cities because they were discriminated against in housing. At this time, it was perfectly lawful for landlords to stipulate 'No Coloureds' or 'No blacks'. Some landlords, like the notorious Peter Rachman, took advantage of the situation by charging overly expensive rents for overcrowded accommodation, which particularly harmed the Afro-Caribbean immigrants who formed the bulk of his tenants.

Source F: An extract from *Bloody Foreigners: The story of immigration to Britain,* by Robert Winder, published in 2004.

> Contrary to the usual insistence on assimilation as a recipe for successful immigration, a high degree of cultural independence seemed to be more useful. An investigation in Nottingham…in the 1960s uncovered a remarkable contrast between the two pioneering groups of immigrants. 87 per cent of Jamaicans said that they felt British before they came; while 86 per cent said it was fine by them if their children 'felt' English. In stark contrast, only 2 per cent of Indians and Pakistanis claimed to feel British before their arrival; and only 6 per cent were willing to accept the idea that their children might feel English. So much for the insistence that immigrants should 'fit in' – the common cry of those outraged by the presence of foreigners in their midst. In practice, those who tried the hardest to fit in were those most actively discouraged from doing so. Those who were able to form their own communities, develop their own economy, and conduct their own affairs – such as Jews, Indians, Pakistanis and Cypriots – found themselves better equipped to advance towards the mainstream.

Source E: A cartoon by Victor Weisz, published in the *Evening Standard,* 19 May 1959.

"THEY JUST AIN'T CIVILISED—LIKE WE ARE . . . !"

Source G: An extract from a news website *Lancaster Unity*. It is describing conditions in the Notting Hill area of London at the time of the 1958 riots.

> Then, the west London neighbourhood as a place of grimy streets and decrepit, overcrowded tenements, a far cry from the chi-chi neighbourhood it is today. The Saturday before the area finally exploded, nine white youths had embarked on what one of them called a 'nigger hunting expedition' around Notting Hill. They were armed with iron bars, blocks of wood, an air pistol and a knife. By the time they'd finished, five black men were in hospital, three in a grave condition.

M. Olden, *The Independent*, Copyright The Independent 29/08/2008.

Follow up more leads

At this stage in your enquiry, you will have a number of leads. You now need to follow them up, using the source file and any other useful sources you have found. Look back at page 44 to keep yourself on track. Review your material – can you identify any gaps which you need to research? What are the key areas that you should go into in more depth? This diagram will help you.

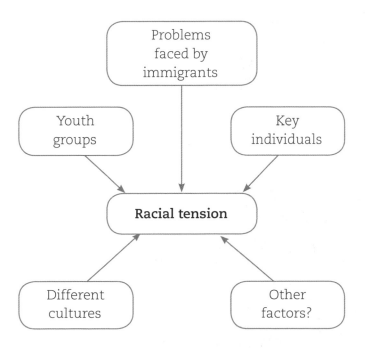

Review and organise material – reach conclusions

Finally, you will need to reach a conclusion. In this example you should decide what were the reasons for the riots in Notting Hill in 1958. You could summarise your key points in a topic web diagram like the one above.

Draw extra arrows to show how the factors link, for example how racist attitudes led to discrimination in housing.

You have found that there are many different opinions on the reasons for the Notting Hill riots in 1958. The task for this enquiry is to show how the various factors combined to lead to riots.

Present your conclusions

This activity gives you practice in presenting the conclusion of your controlled assessment task. After you have completed the activity you could turn to *Maximise your marks* on pages 72–73 to see if your answer could be improved.

Activities

12. Make a set of notes to go with your topic web. Use the same headings. Do not use more than two sides of paper. You can include quotations from your sources in your notes. If you use quotations in your answer, make sure you say who wrote them and also explain why they are important.

13. Write up your enquiry: What were the reasons for the Notting Hill riots in 1958?

ResultsPlus

Top Tip

You will get better marks for your Part A enquiry if you refer specifically to sources that you have read. For example, instead of saying 'some historians', include the actual name of the author. You can also use a short quotation.

Following up an enquiry 2: Changes in the role and status of women – did attitudes towards women in the home change in the years 1955 to 1975?

This practice enquiry is different from enquiry 1. Enquiry 1 asked you to find out why the Notting Hill riots took place in 1958. This enquiry gives you practice in making comparisons and deciding how much attitudes towards the role of women in the home changed in the period 1955–1975.

You want to find out whether attitudes towards women in the home were different in the mid-1970s than in the mid-1950s. Follow the enquiry stages outlined on page 44. Identify, sift and sort your information.

Begin by looking back at pages 15–25 of this book. Then go on to the information given in the source file on pages 50–52.

For example, during the mid-1950s:

- new domestic appliances were targeted at women
- women were still seen as totally responsible for housework.

Activities

14. Read pages 15–25 and the source file. Make a bullet point list of useful information.

15. Begin to organise your notes. You could arrange them into a chart like the one below. Headings have been provided for you. Add key information using bullet points for each heading in the chart.

The role of women in the home in the 1950s	Areas which had changed
• •	• •
The role and status of women in the home in the 1970s	Areas which had not changed
• • •	• •

16. Finally, think about how much change you can see and how important these changes were. Consider whether the changes were:

- major changes that affected a large part of women's daily lives, such as the increasing acceptance of married women going out to work and women as equal to men
- minor ones such as improvements to existing technology and more consumer goods such as washing machines.

Source file

Source A: An extract from *A Sixties Social Revolution? British Society 1959–1975* by S. Waller, published in 2008.

> The belief that the duty of a woman was to be a good wife and mother, keeping a clean home and feeding children and husband, remained strong for most of the 1960s, particularly among the working classes. Women were encouraged to give up their job and personal independence when they married or on the arrival of the first child and, whilst new electrical household appliances and convenience foods might make their life easier, they did not change society's perception of their role.

Source B: Margaret Thatcher interviewed in 1976 for the radio programme *Woman's Hour*.

> I didn't become an MP until after my children had started to go to school because I think that when they are very young they need mum. Mum certainly needs to be with them. Women who do their own job outside the home just have to keep going, in the evenings and at weekends.

Source C: An extract from *White Heat; A History of Britain in the Swinging Sixties*, by Dominic Sandbrook, published in 2006.

By having smaller families, expanding into the workforce and asserting their equal status with men, women participated in British national life as never before. A girl of sixteen in 1970 was far more likely to remain in education than a similar sixteen year old in 1956. She was more likely to pursue her own intellectual and cultural interests for as long as she liked, to marry when and whom she wanted, to have children when and if she wanted, and above all, to choose whether she remained at home as a housewife or pursued her own career. These were not small advances, and they had a profound effect on the way men and women saw themselves. If we are looking for a genuine revolution in the sixties; then perhaps this was it; a revolution with its roots deep in British social history, but a revolution nonetheless.

Source D: A woman teacher interviewed in 1960 quoted in *OCR GCSE Modern World History*, by Ben Walsh, published in 2009.

I was the boss in my kitchen and that is how I liked it. I knew where everything was. My husband never came into the kitchen, so I did all the cooking, all the preparation, all the washing up. He didn't know the first thing about the washing machine, he didn't know the first thing about ironing, and he didn't know the first thing about the cooker. It was my ambition to run the house to the best of my ability. Being a housewife was a twenty-four hour job.

Source E: 'Is there Life after Marriage?' – a poster produced by the 'Why be a wife?' campaign in the 1970s.

WHY BE A WIFE CAMPAIGN, c/o 214 Stapleton Hall Road, London N4.

Source F: British Prime Minister Edward Heath with 13 of the 15 newly elected Conservative women MPs outside the House of Commons in London on 30 June 1970.

Writing up your answer

The moderator will be looking for four main things – that you have:

- kept your answer focused on the enquiry
- found information from different sources
- backed up your statements with information
- communicated your answer by organising it well and using good spelling, punctuation and grammar.

The activities which follow will help you to improve your writing. Remember to use the skills you have learned when you write up your controlled assessment answer.

Activities

Improving writing

17. Study examples 1 and 2 on the next page, imagining you are the moderator. Discuss with a partner the good and bad points of each example. You will find the answers at the bottom of the page.

18. Suggest ways you could improve example 1 and 2. You can do this in bullet point notes.

19. Study example 3. It is part of a high-level response. It looks clearly at changes in attitudes towards women in the home, and gives some specific details and examples to support points that are made. Now try adding to the answer by giving examples to support the last statement. You can also add more paragraphs giving similarities and differences.

Example extract 1

Things did not change that much. Women still had the main role in the home. They still did not have the same sorts of jobs or the same sort of education. They were much the same. They did not have as good jobs as men. Women still did a lot of the work in the home and looked after children.

Example extract 2

Attitudes towards women in the home did begin to change between the 1950s and the 1970s. In the 1950s it was still very much the responsibility of women to look after the home and to care for children. Women were seen as neglecting the home if they worked. Magazines and adverts also showed this traditional view of women. Slowly this began to change. It became more accepted for women to work and to have roles outside of the home. Attitudes take a long time to change but the role of women also changed because of laws passed. This led to things like the Equal Pay Act after a strike by women working in Ford car factories. The Equal Pay Act went some way to improving the lives of women but it was not law straight away because employers needed time to prepare for it Then later laws gave women more rights for maternity pay.

Example extract 3

Attitudes towards women in the home did change between the mid-1950s and the mid-1970s. In the mid-1950s it was clear that the role of women was to be a dutiful housewife and mother. Adverts showed this traditional view of women. This is also shown in publications which aimed to show women how to be successful in looking after their husband and the home [answer quotes from sources]. The advice given is very traditional. Even in the children's reading books, such as 'Janet and John', the message was clearly for girls to work in the kitchen helping with domestic chores.

Interviews with women [answer quotes from sources] show how their role was to look after their husbands and not to think about their own careers. Women were seen as neglecting the home if they worked.

These traditional attitudes started to change by the mid-1970s and there was less opposition to married women also working [answer quotes employment statistics]. Work by historians such as Sandbrook show how women had become more 'assertive' and had begun to 'participate' more in national life. This means that women were gradually having more influence and entering more professions. It had therefore become more acceptable for women to pursue opportunities outside of the home. They were also gradually making advances as we can see from the photograph showing the most women ever elected as Conservative MPs in 1970. Women also had more choices about their home lives, for example many chose to have smaller families. However, the changes did not lead to total equality and women's role in the home had not changed that much. Many women were facing a 'double burden' of still having to do most of the work in the home as well as having to prove themselves in the workplace.

Summary

Success in your enquiry comes from:

- sticking to the focus of the enquiry
- using a range of sources, keeping their relevance and reliability in mind
- organising your answer to show good quality of written communication.

Example 1 does identify some limits to change but it is not detailed enough and it does not identify any differences. It does not refer to any sources.

Example 2 has more detail and has made some comments about similarity and difference. But the student has got side-tracked. The answer starts looking more at the employment of women. Example 2 does not refer to any sources.

Part B Representations of history

'The swinging sixties': an accurate description of Britain in the 1960s?

Learning outcomes

By the end of this chapter, you should be able to:

- describe different aspects of the 'swinging sixties'
- explain the problems historians face in using evidence about the 'swinging sixties'
- explain why historians develop different opinions about the 'swinging sixties'.

In Part B of your controlled assessment you are exploring the use of the term 'swinging' to describe the 1960s. People obviously had different experiences during this period so you need to think about how far it is an appropriate term to use as a label for the 1960s. The aim of this chapter is to explore this issue and understand why historians' views about the 1960s also differ.

This will help you in Part B of the controlled assessment, when you have to evaluate different representations of the sixties.

Watch out

Traditional attitudes were being challenged by young people but the historian also has to understand that many people did not accept these new ideas. The full range of attitudes that existed at the time must be considered.

Activities

1. Copy the topic web about aspects of teenagers' lives in society today and add examples for each of the headings.

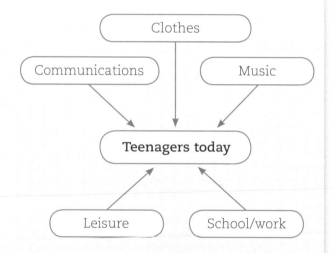

2. Compare your diagram with your neighbour's – what are the similarities? Discuss your ideas as a whole class and add further details to your own summary.
3. Colour-code your diagram to show positive and negative aspects of society today.
4. How different would your diagram be if it were about the life of someone from a minority group, an old person or a business professional instead of a teenager?
5. Using the work you have just done, explain why it is difficult for historians to choose a single term to summarise the whole of society.

'The swinging sixties': an accurate description of Britain in the 1960s?

55

Society in the sixties

The idea of the 'swinging sixties' is linked to:

- rebellion against the stricter values of the older generation
- a sense of freedom, independence and change
- a tolerant attitude towards sex and drugs.

It seemed that Britain, especially London, was leading a cultural revolution which spread across Europe and the USA. The triumphant attitude was also symbolised by the Union Jack flag, which was used on clothes, cars, posters, etc. – especially after England won the football World Cup in 1966!

But the 'swinging' aspect of the sixties seemed to be mainly linked to young adults and centred around London. Historians question how far the rest of the country actually shared these attitudes and experiences.

Source A: Rush hour on Waterloo Bridge in central London, 1964. Notice the 'bubble car' and the mini as well as the double-decker bus that was closely associated with London. This sort of bus featured in Cliff Richard's film *Summer Holiday*.

Did everyone swing in the sixties?

There is no shortage of evidence about the sixties:

- Many people wrote diaries and letters that tell us about their lives.
- There was a range of national and local newspapers.
- Magazines reflected the interests of different groups.
- Many people had cameras to take photographs and even filmed home movies.
- Television was broadcast by the BBC and ITV.
- Sixties music is easily available.

However, despite the large amount of available evidence, historians cannot be sure that the sources show 'typical' life. Newspapers and magazines are far more likely to report exciting new developments in London and the major cities than they are to write about old ideas and fashions continuing in small towns and villages.

Furthermore, new ideas in music and fashion are more likely to be accepted by young people than the older generation. So our evidence may over-emphasise youth culture and the 'London scene', creating the impression that these new ideas were being accepted by the whole of society, throughout the country.

Activities

6. Look at Source A. Explain whether you would use this photograph as evidence for the idea of 'swinging London' in the sixties.

7. The media today often suggest that alcohol, drugs, underage sex and violence are common aspects of teenagers' lives; how accurate do you think this view is and what sources would you use to support your view?

8. Explain how research based on each of the following sources could reach different impressions of what is 'typical' in society today:

   a) The television programmes shown on BBC 1 from 6pm until midnight on a Monday night.

   b) The front page of a popular newspaper for a week.

   c) Your diary, blog, emails or texts for one day.

   d) Photographs from a party or club on a Saturday night.

The dark side

'Swinging sixties' makes it sound as if life was fun for everyone. If you had the money to buy the clothes and the music, and if you lived in London or a major city, then you could feel part of the 'fab scene'. But if you were unemployed or in a job with low pay, living in crowded housing and trying to deal with the problems of poverty, it was a very different experience.

This creates another problem for historians – how can they form an opinion about the sixties when the information seems contradictory?

Poverty

Source B: A photograph by Nick Hedges, 'Mother and children, Balsall Heath, 1969'.

Poverty was a problem for many people during the sixties but issues like this tend to be ignored when only the 'swinging' aspects of society are emphasised. Other evidence creates a more negative impression of the sixties, as is shown in the Fact file on housing in London.

Some people at the time were not aware of the extent of this problem and were shocked by the television programme *Cathy Come Home*, which was screened in 1966 and showed the effects of poverty on family life.

Evidence for the problems of poverty also comes from the organisation Shelter, which was founded in 1966 to help the homeless and commissioned Nick Hedges to travel the country photographing the poor housing conditions.

Fact file

Peter Rachman owned over 100 properties, which he divided into flats. Many of these were in the Notting Hill area of London and were slum properties. However, he was able to charge high rents for them because so many Afro-Caribbean immigrants faced prejudice when they looked for accommodation that they would accept these conditions.

Fact file

Number of children taking free school meals in England and Wales

1960: 247,000

1964: 281,000

1969: 594,000

'The swinging sixties': an accurate description of Britain in the 1960s?

57

Violence and crime

This was also a time of violence. The 'Battle of Brighton' on the May bank holiday of 1964 is estimated to have involved more than 1,000 mods and rockers, and similar clashes occurred at Margate and other resorts on the south coast of England.

Meanwhile, the crime gang led by the Kray twins controlled organised crime in the East End of London throughout most of the 1950s and 1960s. Their tactics included arson, assaults and murder.

Fact file

Approximate number of violent crimes against people

1955: 6,000

1960: 11,000

1969: 21,000

'The most evil woman in Britain'

Between 1963 and 1965, Ian Brady and Myra Hindley kidnapped and murdered five children aged between 10 and 17 in the Greater Manchester area; three of the children are also known to have been sexually assaulted. The bodies were buried on Saddleworth Moor.

Although Brady was the dominant partner, people were particularly shocked at the involvement of a woman in these crimes against children and the press called Myra Hindley 'the most evil woman in Britain'.

'No coloureds'

As you have already seen, many immigrants experienced prejudice and discrimination when they settled in Britain. The race riots in Notting Hill, London, in 1958 were particularly notable (see pages 7–8), but there were many other examples of racial discrimination and Enoch Powell's 'Rivers of Blood' speech (see page 10) shows how the racial tensions remained throughout the sixties.

Source C: A description of the Notting Hill riots, in August 1958, written for *The Guardian* newspaper in 2002.

The disturbances were overwhelmingly triggered by 300- to 400-strong 'Keep Britain White' mobs…The first night left five black men lying unconscious on the pavements of Notting Hill. The battles raged over the bank holiday weekend as the black community responded in kind with counterattacks by large groups of 'men of colour' similarly armed. Thomas Williams was stopped by the police…[and] was found to have a piece of iron down his left trouser leg, a petrol bomb in his right pocket and an open razor blade in his inside breast pocket: 'I have to protect myself,' he told the arresting officer…The disturbances continued night after night until they finally petered out on September 5. At the Old Bailey, Judge Salmon later handed down exemplary sentences of four years each on nine white youths who had gone 'nigger hunting'.

A. Travis, *The Guardian*, 24/08/2002. Copyright Guardian News & Media Ltd 2002.

The 1960s – swinging or suffering?

As you can see, not everyone would have found the sixties to be a 'swinging' time. The problem for historians is that the evidence is contradictory.

Swinging sixties	Suffering sixties
People had money to spend on fashion, music and a social life.	People were very poor, sometimes homeless.
People had tolerant attitudes and different social groups mixed readily with each other.	Afro-Caribbean, Asian and Irish settlers faced prejudice and discrimination.
People had freedom and independence; women had more equality with men.	Women often faced prejudice and discrimination.

It is therefore understandable that historians have different views about the sixties because they focus on different groups within society and come to different conclusions when they weigh the evidence.

Activities

9. What evidence is there of poverty in Source B?

10. How does the information in this section contradict the positive impression of life in the sixties on pages 36–41?

11. Summarise the information on pages 54–58 in a mind map and colour-code positive points green and negative aspects red.

12. Do you think it is easier to find evidence of a 'swinging' society or evidence of the problems of the 1960s? Explain your reasons.

13. Divide the class into two large groups representing positive and negative aspects of society in the sixties. Each large group should then split into smaller groups to research work, housing, entertainment, law and order, and social attitudes in the sixties. Then hold a class debate to decide whether the positive view of the sixties is an accurate one.

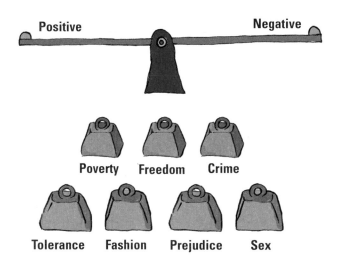

Attitudes and values

The Who's song *My Generation*, which was released in 1965, included the line 'Hope I die before I get old' and in many ways this sums up the rebellious attitude of youth during the 'swinging sixties'. Traditional attitudes were being challenged by young people and the historian has to understand the full range of attitudes that existed at the time.

Sex and scandal

Changes in attitudes towards sex were shown by the availability of the contraceptive pill, the legalisation of abortion and changes to the law on homosexuality. When the publishing company Penguin was put on trial for printing D. H. Lawrence's book *Lady Chatterley's Lover* in 1960, the newspapers ridiculed the prosecution as being out of touch with society.

And yet, Mary Whitehouse, a teacher in the 1960s who opposed the spread of swearing and casual sex, was a hero for many people. She felt that books and magazines, plays, television, etc. had a duty to uphold a high standard of morals and she began a 'Clean Up TV' campaign in 1964. Many people shared her views – she made 300 speeches a year, and in 1964 coaches from around the country brought over 2,000 people to hear her speak in Birmingham, with many more standing outside.

Challenging the establishment

During the Second World War and the 1950s, most people respected authority, but the new spirit of choice and independence during the 1960s led to changes in this relationship. There was genuine concern that a scruffy appearance and long hair was linked to a lack of respect for tradition and authority. However, the Profumo scandal, the trial of Stephen Ward and the BBC programme, *That Was The Week That Was* (or *TW3*), which was broadcast from 1962 to 1963, all showed a decline in respect for authority.

A historian also needs to recognise that values may change over time and that his or her values may be different from those in the sixties. Nowadays, many of our comedians mock **the establishment** and this may make it difficult for historians to appreciate that some people in the sixties were genuinely shocked by the change in attitudes towards authority that was taking place. On the other hand, people today may be shocked by *The Black and White Minstrel Show*, which was a hugely popular television programme in which singers 'blacked up' as African-Americans in a way that people would find offensive now.

The establishment: the groups involved in running the country: the government, the law courts, the police, the church, etc. They tend to hold traditional views and to emphasise law and order.

'The swinging sixties': an accurate description of Britain in the 1960s?

59

Source D: A photograph of singers from *The Black and White Minstrel Show*.

Activities

14. Make a list of the ways musicians influence people's behaviour and attitude, for example do they make drugs and rehab. 'cool'; do they influence our attitudes towards poverty or green issues; do their lyrics and videos influence our attitudes towards swearing, sex, women and violence?

15. From the point of view of people living during the sixties, place the following examples of behaviour in rank order, starting with the most shocking:

    a) In the early sixties, when they first became popular, The Beatles had hair that touched their collars.

    b) Members of The Kinks had an onstage fight in Cardiff in 1965.

    c) The Who smashed their equipment on stage.

    d) In the late sixties, The Beatles took drugs and their song *Lucy in the Sky with Diamonds* was believed to be a reference to the drug LSD.

    e) Mick Jagger and Keith Richards of The Rolling Stones served time in prison for drug possession in 1967.

16. What aspects of the 'swinging sixties' do you think Mary Whitehouse would have wanted to 'clean up'?

17. If historians are not themselves shocked by these aspects of the sixties, do you think they might be tempted to overlook or even ridicule Mary Whitehouse and her supporters?

18. Explain whether a modern historian would find it more difficult to understand people in the sixties being shocked at the length of the Beatles' hair or their acceptance of *The Black and White Minstrel Show*.

19. How do you think historians should deal with the difficulties of writing about groups or events if they have different attitudes and values from the people at the time?

Summary

In the sixties a range of social groups had different experiences. Historians have different views about how 'swinging' the sixties were. This is because:

- Different sources reflect the different experiences of a range of social groups.

- In some cases sources contradict each other.

- Historians must carry out a great deal of research before they can decide what is 'typical'.

- The historian might not share the attitudes and values of people during the sixties.

Study Source D, which shows the cover of another book about the sixties. The centre image is a 'single' – a record containing one musical track on each side; the other images show:

- The Rolling Stones
- a poster advertising the American film *Barbarella*
- Bobby Moore after winning the World Cup
- the Kray twins
- the actor, Michael Caine, reading a newspaper
- The Beatles
- a scene from a James Bond film (a British film)
- the model Twiggy
- Patrick McNee (from *The Avengers*).

Source D: The cover of R*emember the 60s,* published in 2007.

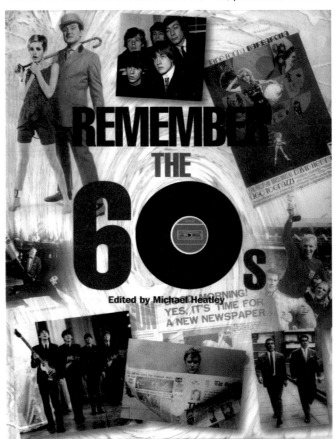

Notice that both covers have shown Bobby Moore, The Beatles and *The Avengers* – this suggests that football, music and television are seen as being an important aspect of the sixties. However, historians need to use in-depth knowledge of the period to decide whether these examples are typical of the period they are being used to represent.

64

Activities

7. The image in Source D contains a reference to crime and violence – how might this suggest that Source D is a more balanced and objective view of the sixties than Source C?

8. Source C has included Harold Wilson, who was Prime Minister for part of the sixties; in what way does this choice suggest that the representation in C covers a wider context than D?

You should now have a clear understanding that an analysis of the differences between two representations should not simply be a list of what is and isn't included in each representation. The analysis should look at the overall attitude and be aware of the decisions involved in creating that particular view.

Source E: A scene from the 1979 film *Quadrophenia* which was about mods in the 1960s.

ResultsPlus
Watch out

Films and television programmes can be very convincing re-creations of the past because the details are so carefully researched. You need to think very carefully about whether the situation and attitudes fit in with your knowledge of the sixties.

Activity

9. Source E is from a film which attempts to recreate certain aspects of life in the sixties. Analyse the image to identify the aspects of the sixties that are being selected to represent the period.

Activity

10. Source E focuses on a single aspect of life in the sixties whereas Sources C and D aim to give an overall 'flavour' of the period. Explain which approach you think is the best way to represent a period.

Analysing written historical representations

Written views of the sixties also create an image through the choice of words, the selection and omission of details and the organisation of the material.

Source F: An extract from *The 1960s, Britain in Pictures*, published in 2008.

> Youth cut loose in the Sixties. They squatted in empty houses and smoked dope. They wore outrageous clothes. They listened to music that, even if it didn't emanate from the devil, was certainly played at a volume that suggested all hell had broken out. They fought. They danced…They had plenty of heroes to choose from – Mary Quant, Twiggy, Jan Palach. Che Guevara, Mick Jagger… DJs, pop stars, footballers, racing drivers, film stars and four lads from Liverpool.

Activities

11. What aspects of youth culture are mentioned in Source F?

12. How does the author of Source F convey the idea that some people at the time did not approve of the activities of youth?

Source G: An extract from *Those were the 60s*, by David Carter, published in 2003.

> Swinging London was at the heart of sexual changes sweeping the country in 1967…Free-love communes were much talked about. Yet outside London and the big cities it could still be difficult to break the rules; many parents wouldn't allow it and it would be hard to find landlords or landladies who were willing to rent a room to an unmarried couple.

Sources F and G are both about youth culture during the sixties but one difference is that Source F is about music, fashion, and youth rebellion, while G is about sex. However, a far more important difference between the two sources is that the two authors have such different views about what was typical of youth culture in the sixties. Source F suggests that the sixties truly were 'swinging' while Source G suggests that 'swinging' only happened in the cities.

The fact that these sources have different views of the situation does not necessarily mean that one of them is wrong. The two authors might simply have used different sources but they might also have used the same sources and reached different conclusions. They might also have chosen to emphasise different aspects of the sixties because they are looking at the period in different ways.

The author of Source F might be basing his work on the situation in London while the author of Source G is aiming to look at the wider context. The author of Source G is also suggesting that many people assume the situation in London was typical of the situation everywhere. He wants to emphasise that this is not true, so consequently his view stresses the other side of the issue and he suggests that an ordinary, 'non-swinging' life was far more typical of the sixties.

Activity

13. Study Sources F and G and then copy and complete the table comparing them.

	Source F	Source G
Aspects of sixties society covered		
Specific details provided		
Attitude – view of 'swinging sixties'		
Key decisions of selection, omission and emphasis that created the overall impression		

Source E: Extracts from *A History of Modern Britain*, by Andrew Marr, published in 2007.

The pop songs of the early Beatles or the Kinks were not…neatly packaged…as all pop songs later became… This innocence extended even to the mistakes – the belief that drugs could make urban life [better].

The majority who lived through the decade have personal memories of rather conventional **suburban** and provincial lives…People did have money in their pockets but it was still being spent on holidays at Butlin's and the seaside rather than on decadent parties…Mothers tended to cook and clean at home…

So in one way the story of 'the sixties'…is elitist. A relatively small number of musicians, entrepreneurs, writers, designers and others created what the rest now study and talk about…If you weren't listening in the Cavern Club in the early days…or [never] sashayed out of Bazaar with a bright bag of swirly-patterned clothes…then sorry, Babe, you missed it, and you missed it for ever. Most of us did miss it – too young, too old, too living-in-the-wrong-place…

Yet…the new culture was far from elitist: it was shaped by working-class and lower-middle-class people… There was a DIY spirit…[Mary Quant took] on the fashion industry of Paris and the West End from a bedsit and a tiny shop…Quant's shockingly short mini-skirts (named after the car, which she loved) were offensive enough for her window to be rapped by umbrella-toting male protestors…She always said she was trying to free women to be able to run for a bus.

> **Suburban:** an area, usually residential, away from the centre of a city, from which people tend to commute.

Andrew Marr is covering a much bigger period than just the sixties. His book goes from the end of the Second World War in 1945 up to 2006, looking at political changes, the economic situation and changes in society. His section on the sixties lasts for over a hundred pages and, within that, he spends ten pages writing about changing attitudes to sex, abortion, homosexuality and the death penalty, five pages about fashion, seven pages about music, three pages about swinging London and three pages about drugs. In other words, only one quarter of his section on the sixties is about the 'swinging scene'.

Activities

8. What criteria has David Carter used in Source D to explain why he thinks the release of The Beatles' first single was a decisive event?

9. Create your own context box to help you evaluate the claims in Source D. You will need to carry out research on the album sales and tours of The Beatles in 1963, 'Beatlemania', and the image of The Beatles compared to the image of The Rolling Stones.

10. Research two of the following (one from List A and one from List B) and create a presentation or hold a class discussion to decide what music was typical of the 'swinging sixties'.

List A	List B
Cilla Black	The Kinks
Sandie Shaw	The Small Faces
The Searchers	Procol Harum

11. Using this knowledge of music during the sixties, explain whether you feel the view in Source D is:
    - accurate   • complete   • objective.

12. Which of the following purposes do you feel best describes Andrew Marr's intentions in the extracts from his book in Source E?
    - To explain what the mood was during the 'swinging sixties'.
    - To challenge the idea of the 'swinging sixties'.

13. Study Source E and give it a rating from 0 to 10 for each of the following criteria:
    - accuracy of the information
    - coverage of the sixties
    - objective approach and language.

ResultsPlus
Watch out

When you evaluate representations you must always explain your criteria. Don't assume that the representation with the most detail is best. Even if that detail is accurate, it may not be very comprehensive, while a representation that is not very objective can still contain accurate detail.

Evaluating representations created by historians

Historians aim to give you their view of past events. They have researched the topic and the details in their writings are likely to be accurate. However, the representation they create is shaped by a number of factors:

- choice of topic
- selection of sources
- evaluation of the evidence
- selection and omission of details in the portrayal
- arrangement and treatment of details in the portrayal which creates a positive or a negative impression, or an emphasis on certain aspects.

Therefore historians aim to be objective in their research but the role of the historian is then to offer an interpretation of events.

Dominic Sandbrook, in Source H on page 66, agrees with Andrew Marr that the 'swinging' aspect of the sixties was focused around London, but Sandbrook emphasises that the attitudes of many people did not change, while Marr says there was a change. Sandbrook is looking at attitudes towards sex while Marr is talking about a general spirit of freedom. They have approached the sixties from different perspectives, which means they can both be giving accurate representations, even though they are different.

Evaluating the focus of the representation

In question B(ii) you are asked to compare three representations and explain which one is 'best'. You have already seen that representations can be evaluated in a number of different ways but an additional point to consider is the focus of the representation.

Is a detailed view of one aspect of the sixties 'better' than an overview of different aspects fitting together?

Look back to Source C where six images have been selected to form an overall representation. This gives us a good overview of the positive side of the 'swinging sixties' but is that more helpful than Source D, which gives us an understanding of what was happening in music?

We also know that there were negative aspects of life in the sixties, which are not shown in Source C.

Think about whether a representation focusing on the 'swinging' aspects of the sixties, which only involved certain groups in society, is 'better' than one which shows the ordinary life of the majority, represented by Dominic Sandbrook's comment in Source H on page 66.

You may also need to consider whether a visual representation is 'better' than a written one. Sources B and E both make the point that some groups were not greatly involved in the 'swinging society' of the sixties but Andrew Marr also suggests that changing attitudes did affect many ordinary people in some way. Which source is more accurate or comprehensive?

ResultsPlus

Top Tip

Remember, two people can come to different judgements about which representation is better and still get the same marks. The important thing is to be able to show that you have used criteria and can back up your decisions using the representations themselves and your own knowledge.

Activity

14. In question B(ii) you have to evaluate three different representations of the 'swinging sixties' and decide which one is best. Read through the Maximise Your Marks section on pages 72–78. Use the mark scheme and the comments to help you write a practice answer evaluating the cartoon in Source B, the jigsaw in Source C and Andrew Marr's views in Source E.

Summary

- A historian's writing aims to be accurate and objective.
- Criteria must always be used when evaluating representations.
- The criteria could be: accuracy, comprehensiveness, objectivity and purpose or focus of the representations.
- Representations must be evaluated in their historical context.

Part A Carry out a historical enquiry

In this task, you are required to carry out an enquiry; the enquiry focus will be set by Edexcel. The task is worth 20 marks and you should aim to spend about an hour writing it up. The mark scheme below shows how your teacher will mark your work for this task. Remember that in this task you are also assessed on the quality of your written communication: use historical terminology where appropriate, organise the information clearly and coherently, and make sure your spelling, punctuation and grammar are accurate.

Level	Answers at this level...	Marks available
Level 1	Make simple comments. There are few links between them and few details are given. Only one or two sources have been used in the enquiry.	1–5 marks
Level 2	Make statements about the enquiry topic. Information is included that is mostly relevant and accurate, but it is not well organised to focus on the point of the enquiry. A range of sources has been consulted and information taken from them.	6–10 marks
Level 3	Are organised to focus mainly on the point of the enquiry. Accurate and relevant information is given to support the points the student makes. A range of sources has been found and well-chosen material taken from them.	11–15 marks
Level 4	Focus well on the point of the enquiry. A well-supported conclusion is reached, for example about: the nature of change OR whether one factor was more important than the others OR the inter-relationship between two or more of the factors (depending on the enquiry focus). A range of sources appropriate to the enquiry has been identified and material from the sources has been well deployed.	16–20 marks

Let's look at an extract from one student's response to the following enquiry:

- The reasons for the Notting Hill riots in 1958

Student response

In the 1950s there were racial tensions. This was because more people were moving to Britain. They were moving to city areas and often in the poorer areas. Many were emigrating to Britain from the Caribbean and from southern Asia. They found it hard to find places to live and to find jobs. There were tensions between them and the white people. The immigrants sometimes found it hard to pay their rent. At this time there were no laws to protect them and no laws to stop racism so people sometimes said that black people could not rent their flats. Because there were no laws about racism it was not illegal to put signs up for rooms to rent which said 'No coloureds'. There was also tension between them and the working-class 'Teddy Boys' who were white young men. The white men and the black men also found it hard to get along because the immigrants were seen as taking the Teddy Boys' girlfriends away from them. The white men also felt that the immigrants were taking their jobs away from them. Many people also believed things that they read in the newspapers about what immigrants did. People like Bernie Grant tell us about their experiences when they came to England and about how much racism there was. All of these problems linked together and so led to the riots in Notting Hill.

Moderator comment

This extract indicates that the response would gain a mark in level 2. The student describes the situation facing many immigrants but many of the comments made are undeveloped.

It is not obvious that the student has used a good range of sources. Text books, internet sites and other sources could have been used to provide information, but only Bernie Grant has been quoted. However, relevant material has been included, but this is rather general in nature. To improve the response, the student should focus more centrally on the precise enquiry – the reasons for the Notting Hill riots in 1958 – and so focus on specific events in Notting Hill and the importance of specific factors that led to the Notting Hill riots.

Let's look at an extract from an improved student response.

Improved student response

Race relations in many parts of Britain were bad by the 1950s and in some inner cities there was concern at what was called 'white-flight'. Long-term social problems were made worse by immigration, for example there were problems in housing. Immigrants were resented when some landlords evicted white tenants and let their properties out again at much higher rents to immigrants from the 'New Commonwealth'. Other accommodation displayed notices such as 'No coloureds'. This obviously increased resentment and racial tensions in these inner city areas where the immigrants were. There were other social tensions apart from housing. Many of the young black men were single. Young working-class white males resented young black men if they seemed to be taking 'their' women. The young black men had also developed their own distinct culture with their own bars and music. That made it harder for the black and white communities to integrate.

Economic reasons were another factor in increasing racial tensions. Many people blamed the arrival of immigrants as a reason for rising unemployment. Moreover, some people felt that the immigrants were simply coming to Britain to get welfare benefits and to live off the state.

When some newspapers sensationalised racial tensions and wrote racist and inflammatory articles, this made the situation worse. For example…[answer quotes from sources].

But why did this lead to riots in Notting Hill when there were not riots in every area? Notting Hill was one area where racial tensions were reaching a critical point by the late 1950s because all these various factors combined there. It had a large immigrant community. A strong Caribbean community had gradually developed since the end of the Second World War. There was much poverty in the area among both the white and the black populations. Groups of white 'Teddy Boys' began showing open anger towards local black families. Additionally right-wing fascist groups, such as Oswald Mosley's Union Movement, set up branches in the area and their campaigns encouraged white resentment. They printed leaflets and painted slogans on walls saying 'Keep Britain white'. (This is quoted on the 'Exploring 20th Century London Museums' website.) It was probably this factor which meant that tension in the area turned into open violence.

The riots began when a large group of white (mainly) men started openly attacking black immigrants. As many as 400 white youths were involved. The riots lasted for two weeks. Groups of young white males attacked black groups and black homes. They even used petrol bombs. Violence developed further as some black people retaliated.

Overall the riots began in Notting Hill for a combination of reasons…but the factor which turned resentment into open violence was that fascist groups in the area stirred up tensions and this encouraged violent Teddy Boy groups to attack black people.

Part B(i) Compare two representations

In this task, you are required to analyse and compare two representations of history. The task is worth 10 marks and you should aim to spend about 30 minutes writing it up. The mark scheme below shows how your work for this task will be marked.

Level	Answers at this level…	Marks available
Level 1	Identify the main features of the two representations by giving descriptions, direct quotations or paraphrases from one or both representations.	1–3 marks
Level 2	Identify the differences in the two representations by comparing similarities and/or differences in their details.	4–7 marks
Level 3	Show understanding of the similarities and/or differences in the way the past is represented in the two extracts. The answer uses precisely selected detail from the two representations to support the explanations and the judgement about how far the representations differ.	8–10 marks

Let's look at an extract from one student's response.

- Study Source D on page 64 and Source H on page 66. They are both representations of Britain in the 'swinging sixties'. How far do these representations differ? (10 marks)

Student response

These two representations are about very different aspects of the sixties. The idea of the 'swinging sixties' is linked to changes in fashion and music, usually in London. It is also about youth culture and rebellion against traditional attitudes. Representation D shows many of these things. It has a picture of The Rolling Stones, who were a rebellious music group, The Beatles, who were probably the most famous of the bands in the sixties, and the model Twiggy. It does contain some other images but they are mainly positive ones. It is only the picture of the Kray twins which shows the bad side of the sixties. Representation H is very different because it is all about attitudes and it is saying that attitudes did not really change very much. In particular, it is saying that attitudes remained the same about key issues where the law changed during the sixties, such as sex. So, in a way, Representation H is contradicting Representation D and the representations differ completely.

Results Plus
Maximise your marks

Moderator comment

In this answer the student has understood the details in the representations and has begun to compare them. The student identifies the mainly positive image of the sixties created by Representation D and supports this by referring to specific details and then makes a comparison with Representation H. A link is made between both sources about changing attitudes during the sixties, and the judgement is offered that the representations differ completely and Representation H contradicts Representation D.

There is enough comprehension and comparison for the answer to get into level 2, but the answer concentrates mainly on differences in details and it tends to treat the two representations separately. To raise the response to the next level, the answer should show more awareness of the differences in the portrayal of the sixties. Representation D's focus is on the 'swinging sixties', which is portrayed through famous faces. Representation H's focus is on how far the ideas of the 'swinging sixties' spread throughout society and suggests that these changes in attitude were actually very limited. The fact that different details are used in the two representations is less important than the way Representation D suggests all aspects of society were affected by the 'swinging sixties' while Representation H says that the changes had very limited impact.

Let's look at an extract from an improved student response.

Improved student response

Representations D and H are about very different aspects of the sixties. The idea of the 'swinging sixties' is linked to changes in fashion and music, usually focused on London. This is shown by the pictures of Twiggy, The Rolling Stones and The Beatles. Representation D mainly focuses on popular culture but the way it shows football, television, film, a new newspaper and even the Kray twins, who were criminals but mixed with famous people, all suggests a period which was different and more exciting than the fifties. Although Representation H does not mention any of these aspects of popular culture, it does talk about the sixties being an era of social and cultural change. It also talks about changing attitudes to sex, which was closely linked to the idea of the 'swinging sixties'. Therefore both representations recognise that this was a period of great change, even though they look at different aspects of the sixties.

However, the focus of Representation H is that attitudes did not really change very much. In particular, it is saying that attitudes often remained the same about key issues where the law changed during the sixties, such as sex. So, although the two representations are focusing on different aspects of the sixties, the biggest difference between them is their attitude to the period. Representation D shows the sixties as exciting and mainly positive by emphasising English football triumph, successful pop bands, successful actors, a new newspaper, etc. Representation H plays down the extent of change and new elements by stressing that these changes in attitude did not always reach provincial areas and were sometimes resisted.

Therefore these two representations are very different in several ways. Even though they both recognise that there were many changes in society and culture, Representation D focuses just on the 'swinging' aspects of society and youth culture, whereas Representation H takes a more overall approach, looking at the whole of society, not just the 'in crowd' based around London. For this reason, Representation D stresses the new and popular aspects of culture in the sixties whereas Representation H stresses the continuity and lack of change in attitudes. To some extent they are not just about different aspects of society. Representation H actually undermines the assumption in Representation D that everyone was involved in the 'swinging sixties'.

Part B(ii) Analyse and evaluate three representations

In this task, you are required to analyse and evaluate three representations of history. The task is worth 20 marks and you should aim to spend about an hour writing it up. The mark scheme below shows how your work for this task will be marked. Remember that in this task you are also assessed on the quality of your written communication: use historical terminology where appropriate, organise the information clearly and coherently, and make sure your spelling, punctuation and grammar are accurate.

Level	Answers at this level…	Marks available
Level 1	Show an understanding of the main features of the sources and select material. Simple judgements are made about the representation, and a limited amount of accurate information about the period is given. The material is mostly generalised, and links to the representation are not explicit.	1–5 marks
Level 2	Show an understanding of the main features of the three sources and select key features of the representations from them. Judgement is made about the best representation and there is detailed and accurate material about the period, but with little linkage between description and judgement. Judgements may relate to the accuracy or comprehensiveness of the representation.	6–10 marks
Level 3	Analyse the three sources and show some of the ways in which the past situation has been represented. Detail from the sources is used to support the analysis. There is a critical evaluation of the representation based on well selected information about the period and at least two clear criteria are applied, for example the author's purpose or objectivity, or the comprehensiveness and/or accuracy of the representation.	11–15 marks
Level 4	Analyse the three sources to show the way in which the past situation has been represented. Precisely selected detail from the sources is used to support the analysis. There is a critical evaluation of the representation based on precisely selected information about the period and applying at least three criteria, for example the author's purpose or objectivity, or the comprehensiveness and/or accuracy of the representation.	16–20 marks

Let's look at an extract from one student's response to the representations.

- Study Source D on page 64, Source H on page 66 and Source B on page 68.

  Choose the one which you think is the best representation of Britain in the 'swinging sixties'. Explain your choice. You should use all three representations and your own knowledge to explain your answer. (20 marks)

ResultsPlus
Maximise your marks

Student response

All three representations are good in different ways. Representation D shows us some of the key people who made up the 'swinging sixties'. Fashion and music were two very important elements of the 'swinging' scene so the pictures of Twiggy and The Beatles are very important parts of Representation D. The author of Representation D has also included The Rolling Stones, which reminds us that there were different styles of music that were popular. It also shows that rebellion was an aspect of youth culture at this time. Representation D is also useful because it has a picture of the Kray twins and this is a reminder that the period was not entirely a positive one for everyone.

Representation H is very good because it shows us that ideas and attitudes are often slow to change. However, it is very limited and doesn't mention most of the things associated with the 'swinging sixties' so it is less useful than Representation D.

Representation B is also a useful reminder that the ideas and changes of the 1960s didn't reach many people but it gives us very little detail and because it is a cartoon it is not very accurate or reliable.

Representation H does give us some very accurate details but Representation D is the most comprehensive because it covers so many different aspects of the sixties, therefore Representation D is best.

Moderator comment

The student has made various comments about each of the three representations which identify the information they can provide. The answer also makes some comparisons between the representations and begins to use some criteria to evaluate the representations but none of the comments are developed very far. There is the statement that the details in Representation H are accurate but there is no discussion of how to test this accuracy or use of own knowledge to examine the accuracy of any of the representations. Representation B is largely dismissed on the basis of its nature as a cartoon with no consideration of the ways that a cartoon often reflects popular views on key issues.

Representation D is chosen as best because it is seen as being most comprehensive and this is an important criterion to use but the answer would be much stronger if the candidate focused on the spirit and attitudes of the sixties rather than a checklist of topics that should be included. Once again, contextual knowledge is needed in order to establish how far the 'London scene' should be taken as typical of the period. An interesting judgement could be made about whether a representation of the sixties should focus on the limited sections of society involved in the 'swinging scene' or focus on the more widespread ordinary lives of the majority of the population. The answer could also discuss whether the focus of the 'swinging sixties' was cultural or social.

Several of these ideas are touched on but this needs to be done more systematically if the answer is to reach the highest level — three criteria should be used to rate each representation.

Let's look at an extract from an improved student response.

Improved student response

Representation D shows us a range of key people who have been selected as typical of the 'swinging sixties'. It is not possible to have comprehensive coverage but these have been well selected because fashion and music were two very important elements of the 'swinging' scene so the pictures of the model, Twiggy, and The Beatles are very important parts of Representation D. The fact that The Rolling Stones are also included suggests that music is very important but also shows that there was a wide spectrum of popular music. Television and film are also included, the achievement of England winning the World Cup and the launch of a new newspaper. Meanwhile the inclusion of the Kray twins reminds us that the period was not entirely a positive one for everyone. This is therefore fairly comprehensive as it covers both good and bad aspects of the sixties and shows several aspects of popular culture. It does not include Mary Quant's mini, 'flower power' or mods and rockers but it does capture the positive spirit of the sixties.

However, it is not clear whether this positive spirit is actually an accurate view of the sixties. Writers such as Andrew Marr in his book *A History of Modern Britain* and Dominic Sandbrook in *White Heat* stress that life went on as normal for most people. In fact, films such as *Cathy Come Home*, *A Taste of Honey* and *Up the Junction* all stressed the problems of poverty that many working-class families faced, both in the industrial cities of northern England and also in London itself. Representation D is the cover of a book which is not a serious history book and does not claim to survey the whole of society or the whole period. It is a book for entertainment and for people looking back to the sixties, so it is not likely to stress the negative side of life in the sixties. Therefore this representation gives a fairly comprehensive view of the key aspects of the 'swinging sixties' but it does not intend to give an accurate and comprehensive view of the sixties.

Representation H is far less comprehensive in its coverage of aspects of the 'swinging sixties' but it is more accurate as a reflection of the experiences and attitudes of the whole of society…

Representation B is less obviously useful because it has so few details about the sixties. However, cartoons tend to reflect the views of the newspaper readers and this suggests that a number of people would understand the message that the spirit of the sixties was about freedom and tolerance but that many people remained prejudiced. The bowler hat, suit and umbrella are a stereotype of a professional businessman. The cartoon suggests that the new attitudes only affected certain groups of society and this is probably true – the 'swinging sixties' was about youth culture and rebellion against the older generation. So, although this has very few details, the cartoon does include suggestions about the type of changes going on in the sixties and the fact that these changes only had a limited impact. It is therefore fairly accurate and it is comprehensive in the way it includes both sides of the issue. Because it is a cartoon it makes a joke about the men celebrating the fact that they haven't been affected by the sixties but this fits in with programmes such as *Till Death Do Us Part* and the restrictions placed on the changes in the laws on the contraceptive pill and the legalisation of homosexuality.

Glossary

Apartheid: separateness of races – a system of racial segregation used in South Africa between 1948 and 1993.

Black Power: a political slogan and a movement of people of Black African descent that grew out of the civil rights movement in America in the 1960s and 1970s. While it sought political and social equality it also emphasised racial pride in black culture and identity.

Colonies: territories which were part of the British Empire.

Commonwealth: after gaining independence, some former British colonies joined this association. 'New Commonwealth' referred to the mainly non-white and developing areas of the British Commonwealth in Africa and Asia, and 'Old Commonwealth' to areas such as Canada, Australia and New Zealand, which had gained independence earlier.

Decriminalisation: legislation that makes something legal that was formerly illegal.

European Economic Community: often called the 'Common Market' and now the European Union (EU), this was, and is, an organisation designed to bring European states together into a single economic market.

Fascist: relating to a political movement or party which believes that nation and race are more important than the individual. Fascist systems have an all-powerful central government and an authoritarian leader.

Feminism: a movement and set of beliefs aimed at achieving political, social and economic equality of women with men.

Franchise: the right to vote in both local and national government elections.

Hire purchase: paying an initial deposit for items (such as furniture, cars or clothes) followed by monthly payments with interest over an agreed period.

Home Secretary: the government minister in charge of the Home Office of the United Kingdom, who is responsible for many important issues such as policing, immigration and national security.

Icon: something which sums up the mood of the time; it can be used as a symbol for the period.

Legislation: laws made by a government or ruling body.

Liberalisation: the relaxation of previous restrictions, whether by government or society in general.

Nuclear family: a family unit of two married parents and their children in one household.

Primary immigration: refers to a person moving to Britain alone. If members of their family join them later, this is called secondary immigration.

Private Member's Bill: proposed laws introduced by individual MPs rather than the government.

Provincial: relating to parts of the country away from cities such as London and very large centres of population.

Suburban: an area, usually residential, away from the centre of a city, from which people tend to commute.

The establishment: the groups involved in running the country: the government, the law courts, the police, the church, etc. They tend to hold traditional views and to emphasise law and order.

Voluntary repatriation: when individuals choose to return to the country of their origin of their own free will. It may be organised with or without the government's assistance.

Youth culture: the fashions and trends popular among young people.

Published by Pearson Education Limited, a company incorporated in England and Wales, having its registered office at Edinburgh Gate, Harlow, Essex, CM20 2JE. Registered company number: 872828

Edexcel is a registered trademark of Edexcel Limited

Text © Pearson Education Limited

The rights of Nigel Bushnell and Cathy Warren have been asserted by them in accordance with the Copyright, Designs and Patents Act 1988.

First published 2010

12 11
10 9 8 7 6 5 4 3

British Library Cataloguing in Publication Data
A catalogue record for this book is available from the British Library

ISBN 978 1 846906 44 2

Designed and typeset by Juice Creative Ltd, Hertfordshire

Original illustrations © Pearson Education Ltd 2010

Printed in Great Britain at Scotprint, Haddington

Acknowledgements
We would like to thank Dr Christopher Prior for his invaluable help in the development of this material.

Picture credits
The publisher would like to thank the following for their kind permission to reproduce their photographs:

(Key: b-bottom; c-centre; l-left; r-right; t-top)
Reproduced with kind permission of FPA © 2010: 33; **Alamy Images**: Trinity Mirror / Mirrorpix 10; **Apple Corps Ltd.** ; : 40/2; **Koninklijke Jumbo B.V.:** © Getty Images, © Image Estate, © Bridgeman Art Library 69; **BBC Photo Library:** 59; Archive of the Irish in Britain: 6; **Corbis:** 32; **Getty Images:** Keystone / Hulton Archive 24, Bob Aylott 22, John Franks 8, Roger Jackson 52, Joseph McKeown 30, Express Newspapers 7, Bentley Archive / Popperfoto 43, Evening Standard 11; **Nick Hedges:** 56; **HistoryTalk:** Geoff Walley 13; **Kobal Collection Ltd:** CURBISHLEY-BAIRD 64; **Angela Leonard:** 61; **The Women's Library:** 51; **Mirrorpix:** 41, 42; **Museum of London:** Henry Grant Collection 39, Roger Mayne 55; **Photolibrary. com:** Rod Edwards / Britain on View 60; **Punch Cartoon Library:** Hector Breeze 68; **Rex Features:** CLIVE DIXON 20; **Solo Syndication / Associated Newspapers Ltd:** Vicky / The British Cartoon Archive, University of Kent 48; **Museum of Technology:** 40; **TfL from the London Transport Museum collection** : 5; **The Advertising Archives:** 17; **TopFoto:** 28; **www. cartoonstock.com:** Jim Sizemore 16

Cover images: Front: **Getty Images:** Evening Standard/Stringer

All other images © Pearson Education

Every effort has been made to trace the copyright holders and we apologise in advance for any unintentional omissions. We would be pleased to insert the appropriate acknowledgement in any subsequent edition of this publication.

We are grateful to the following for permission to reproduce copyright material:

Screenshots

Screenshot on page 64 from *Remember the 60s*, 978-1-9050-0964-0, Green Umbrella Publishing (Michael Heatley 2006), copyright © G2 Entertainment; Screenshot on page 63 from *White Heat: A History of Britain in the Swinging Sixties, 978-0349118208*, 2, Abacus (Dominic Sandbrook 2007), with permission from Little, Brown Book Group.

Text
Extract on page 12 adapted from The Bernie Grant Archive, Bishopsgate Institute; Extract on page 17 from *The New Look*, published by Secker and Warburg (Hopkins, H. 1964) pp. 325-26, Used by permission of The Random House Group Ltd; Extract on page 19 from Peter and Jane series: *Things we do*, B000MINAHU page 6–7, author William Murray, 1964 Ladybird, Copyright © Penguin Books Ltd; Extract on page 29 adapted from Houses of shame, *The Guardian*, 31/10/2007 (Paton, M.), Copyright Guardian News & Media Ltd. 2007; Extract on page 37 adapted from Mookychick, http://www.mookychick.co.uk/style/history-of-the-miniskirt.php, reprinted with permission from Mookychick.co.uk; Extract on page 42 from 1968: I was there, *The Guardian*, 21/05/2008 (Henley, J.), Copyright Guardian News & Media Ltd. 2008; Extract on page 42 from *The New Encyclopaedia of Brighton* by Rose Collis, published by Brighton & Hove Libraries, 2010; Extracts on page 46, page 51 from *OCR GCSE Modern World History 3rd edition*, published by Hodder Education (Walsh, B. 2009), Copyright © 2009. Reproduced by permission of Hodder and Stoughton Limited; Extract on page 47 from interview with Loftus Burton after the Notting Hill riots, recorded in 1958 Remembered - Riot Reminiscence, http://www.historytalk.org/Notting%20Hill%20History%20 1958/fiftyeightweb2.pdf, with permission from HISTORYtalk; Extract on page 48 from HISTORYtalk Newsletter, Issue 11, May 2008, http:// www.historytalk.org/Newsletter/Newsletter11.pdf, with permission from Historytalk; Extract on page 48 from *OCR Modern World History*, Heinemann (Brodkin, A., Carrington, E., Hill, A., Kerridge, R., Lacrey, G., Marriott, B. 2009) p. 334, with permission from Pearson Education Ltd; Extract on page 48 adapted from *Bloody Foreigners: The story of immigration to Britain*, Little, Brown (Winder, R. 2004) p. 275, Copyright © Robert Winder 2004, with permission from Little, Brown Book Group and Toby Eady Associates on behalf of the author; Extract on page 49 from White riot: The week Notting Hill exploded, *The Independent* (Olden, M.), Copyright The Independent 29/08/2008; Extracts on page 51, page 66 from *White Heat: 1964-1970 A History of Britain in the Swinging Sixties* Abacus (Sandbrook, D. 2007), with permission from Little, Brown Book Group; Extract on page 57 from After 44 years secret papers reveal truth about five nights of violence in Notting Hill, The Guardian, 24/08/2002 (Travis, A.), Copyright Guardian News & Media Ltd. 2002; Extract on page 65 adapted from *The 1960s, Britain in Pictures (Twentieth Century in Pictures)*, Ammonite (PA Photos 2008), with permission from Ammonite Press; Extract on page 70 from *A History of Modern Britain*, Pan Macmillan, London (Marr, A. 2007), Copyright © Andrew Marr, 2007, with permission from Pan Macmillan.

In some instances we have been unable to trace the owners of copyright material, and we would appreciate any information that would enable us to do so.

Extract on page 38 adapted from The story of the mini, http://www.icons. org.uk/theicons/collection/the-mini/biography/the-mini-biography-finished.
Extract on page 50 from *Woman's Hour – Celebrating 60 Years of Women's Lives*, John Murray/Hodder Headline (Murray, J., ed. 2006).
Extract on page 50 from *A Sixties Social Revolution? British Society 1959-1975*, Nelson Thornes (Waller, S. 2009) p. 85.
Extracts on page 65, page 69 from *Those were the 60s* Simon & Schuster (Carter, D. 2003).

Websites
The websites used in this book were correct and up to date at the time of publication. It is essential for tutors to preview each website before using it in class so as to ensure that the URL is still accurate, relevant and appropriate. We suggest that tutors bookmark useful websites and consider enabling students to access them through the school/college intranet.

Disclaimer
This material has been published on behalf of Edexcel and offers high-quality support for the delivery of Edexcel qualifications. This does not mean that the material is essential to achieve any Edexcel qualification, nor does it mean that it is the only suitable material available to support any Edexcel qualification. Edexcel material will not be used verbatim in setting any Edexcel examination or assessment. Any resource lists produced by Edexcel shall include this and other appropriate resources.

Copies of official specifications for all Edexcel qualifications may be found on the Edexcel website: www.edexcel.com